ENGLISH MEN OF LETTERS
EDITED BY JOHN MORLEY

FANNY BURNEY
(MADAME D'ARBLAY)

FANNY BURNEY

(MADAME D'ARBLAY)

BY

AUSTIN DOBSON

New York
THE MACMILLAN COMPANY
LONDON: MACMILLAN & CO., LTD.
1903

PREFACE

THE main sources for this memoir of Frances or Fanny Burney, — afterwards Madame D'Arblay, — in addition to her novels, the literature of the period, and the works specified in the footnotes, are as follows: —

1. *Memoirs of Dr. Burney, arranged from his own Manuscript, from Family Papers, and from Personal Recollections.* By his Daughter, Madame D'Arblay. In Three Volumes. London: Moxon, 1832.

2. *Diary and Letters of Madame D'Arblay*, Author of "Evelina," "Cecilia," etc. Edited by her Niece. [In Seven Volumes.] London: Colburn, 1842–46. [The edition here used is Swan Sonnenschein's four volume issue of 1892.]

3. *The Early Diary of Frances Burney*, 1768–1778. *With a Selection from her Correspondence, and from the Journals of her Sisters Susan and Charlotte Burney.* Edited by Annie Raine Ellis. In Two Volumes. London: George Bell and Sons, 1889.

I am indebted to the kindness of Archdeacon Burney, Vicar of St. Mark's, Surbiton, for access to his unique extra-illustrated copy of the *Diary and Letters* of 1842–6, which contains, among other interesting Mss., the originals of Mrs. Thrale's letter mentioned at page 86 of this volume, and of Burke's letter mentioned at page 124. Archdeacon Burney is the possessor of Edward Burney's portrait of his cousin (page 88); of the Reynolds portraits of Dr. Burney and Garrick from the Thrale Gallery (page 94); of a very fine portrait of Dr. Charles Burney by Lawrence; and of a group by Hudson of Hetty Burney, her husband, Charles Rousseau Burney, and her husband's father, Richard Burney of Worcester.

I am also indebted to Mrs. Chappel of East Orchard, Shaftesbury, granddaughter of Mrs. Barrett, the editor of the *Diary and Letters*, for valuable information as to Burney relics in her possession.

A. D.

75, Eaton Rise, Ealing, W.,
    September 18, 1903.

CONTENTS

FANNY BURNEY

CHAPTER I

THE BURNEY FAMILY

In the second half of the seventeenth century, there lived at the village of Great Hanwood, four miles from Shrewsbury, a country gentleman of a good estate, named James Macburney. In later life, he was land-steward to the Earl of Ashburnham; and he rented or possessed a house in the Privy Garden at Whitehall. Tradition traces his family to Scotland, whence it was said to have arrived with James I. However this may be, — and the point was not regarded as of much importance by his descendants, — James Macburney married his Shropshire rector's daughter; begat a son; and in due time, became a widower. The son — also James Macburney — was educated at Westminster School under the redoubtable Dr. Busby. Then, taking to art, he worked as a pupil of the "eminent Face Painter," Michael Dahl. About 1697, at the age of nineteen, he ran away with Rebecca Ellis, an actress in Giffard's Company, and younger than himself. Thereupon his irate father disinherited him, and in further token of his displeasure, took to wife his own cook, by whom he had another son called Joseph, who, as soon

as he arrived at man's estate, removed all possible
difficulties in regard to the succession by dissipating
the property. Having effected this with much promp-
titude, he settled down contentedly as a Norfolk
dancing master. Meanwhile, his elder half-brother, —
who, though lacking in discretion, had many pleasing
gifts (he was, in particular, an accomplished violin-
player), — being left, by the death of his actress-wife,
with a numerous family, wedded, for the second
time, a beautiful young lady of Shropshire, Mistress
(*i.e.* Miss) Ann Cooper. Miss Cooper was currently
reported to have rejected Wycherley the dramatist,
who, it may be remembered, like the elder Macburney,
was desirous of disappointing his natural heir. Miss
Cooper had some money ; but James Macburney's
second marriage increased the number of his children.
The youngest members of his family were twins,
Susannah (who died early), and Charles, afterwards
the well-known historian of music, and the father of
Fanny Burney. Like his predecessors, he was born
Macburney, but the " Mac " was subsequently dropped.

Not long after Charles Burney's birth, which took
place on the 12th April 1726, in Raven Street, Shrewsbury (a name probably derived from the famous Raven
Inn once familiar to Farquhar and "Serjeant Kite "),
James Burney, as we may now call his father, settled
at Chester as a portrait painter, leaving his little son
at nurse in Condover, a village near Shrewsbury.
Here, with an affectionate foster mother, Charles
Burney throve apace, until he was transferred to the
Chester Grammar School. At this date his natural
gifts were sufficiently manifest to enable him at a
pinch to act as deputy for the Cathedral organist.

Subsequently, he became the pupil of his half-brother, James, the organist of St. Margaret's at Shrewsbury. Then, being again in Chester when the famous Dr. Augustine Arne was passing through the town on his return from Ireland to London, he was fortunate enough to be taken as that master's apprentice. This was in August 1744, when he was eighteen, pleasant-mannered, intelligent, very musical, very versatile, and — as he continued to be through life — an indefatigable worker. From Arne he did not learn much except to copy music, and to drudge in the Drury Lane Orchestra, which Arne conducted; and, although he had an elder brother in London, he was left greatly to his own devices. But his abilities and personal charm brought him many friends. He was frequently at the house in Scotland Yard of Arne's sister, Mrs. Cibber, the foremost tragic actress of her day; and here he made acquaintance with many notabilities. Handel was often among the visitors, playing intricate fugues and overtures with his pudgy fingers upon the harpsichord; and Garrick, with the wonderful eyes; and Garrick's surly old rival, the *bon-vivant*, James Quin; and Mason; and Thomson the poet of *The Seasons*.

With Arne, Charles Burney would probably have remained, but for a fortunate accident. At the shop of Jacob Kirkman, the German harpsichord-maker in Broad Street, Golden Square, he met Mr. Fulke Greville, a descendant of Sidney's friend, the famous Fulke Greville of Queen Elizabeth's days. The Greville of 1746 either possessed, or affected to possess, many of the attributes of Bramston's *Man of Taste*: —

> "I would with *Jockeys* from *Newmarket* dine,
>   And to *Rough-riders* give my choicest wine . . .
> In *Fig* the Prize-fighter by day delight,
>   And sup with *Colly Cibber* ev'ry night."

Like Bramston's hero, he also dabbled in gardening.
But his accomplishments were not confined to pugilism
and field sports. He danced, fenced, drew, wrote
verses, and trifled with metaphysics. Lastly, he "*had
an ear.*" After the fashion of his day, he had doubted
whether any musician could possibly be a gentleman,
but Charles Burney undeceived him. The result was
that Greville paid three hundred pounds to cancel
Burney's engagement to Arne, and attached his new
friend to his own establishment in the capacity of
musical companion. This curious conjunction, which
seems to have included a fair experience of Greville's
other diversions, did no harm to Charles Burney. On
the contrary, at Greville's country seat of Wilbury
House in Wiltshire, he met many interesting and some
eminent people, who considerably enlarged his social
aptitudes. In 1747, however, his patron married a
Miss Frances Macartney, — the "Flora" of Horace
Walpole's *Beauties*, — making, in his impatience of the
conventional, — or *fogrum* as it was then styled, — a
perfectly superfluous stolen match. "Mr. Greville"
— said the lady's matter-of-fact father, when his pardon
and blessing were formally requested — "has chosen to
take a wife out of the window, whom he might just as
well have taken out of the door." Burney gave away
the bride ; and after standing proxy for a duke at the
baptism of the first child,[1] would have accompanied

[1] This was Fanny Burney's later friend, — the beautiful Mrs.
Crewe of Reynolds, and the "Amoret" of Sheridan and Charles
Fox.

the Grevilles to Italy. But at this juncture he discovered that he, too, had an affair of the heart. Thereupon Mr. Greville magnanimously released him from his engagement, and left him to marry the woman of his choice.

She was a Miss Esther Sleepe, very attractive and very amiable. Her mother, although of Huguenot origin, was a Roman Catholic. Esther herself was a Protestant. She married Charles Burney about 1748, and they went to live in the City. In 1749, her husband was appointed organist of St. Dionis Backchurch, which had been rebuilt by Wren after the Great Fire. Burney's modest salary was £30 per annum. But he composed music, and soon found many pupils. When his first child, called Esther after her mother, was born, is not stated; but the register of St. Dionis contains record of the birth, in June, 1750, of James Burney, afterwards an admiral; and, in 1751, of a son Charles, who, apparently, died early. Before this date, hard work and close application had begun to tell upon the father of the little family, and he was advised by his friend Dr. John Armstrong, the author of *The Art of Preserving Health*, to try living in the country. He accordingly accepted the post of organist, with a salary of £100 a year, at St. Margaret's Church, King's Lynn, to which place he removed in 1751, his wife joining him some months later. At King's Lynn, on the 13th June 1752, was born his second daughter, Frances, or Fanny Burney, whose life-story forms the theme of this volume. The name of Frances came to her from her godmother, Mrs. Greville; and she was baptized at St. Nicholas, in Ann Street. At Lynn were born two other children, Susanna, no doubt so named after

her father's twin sister; and a second Charles, later a
famous Greek scholar, Rector of Deptford, and Chaplain to George III. The date of Susanna's birth is
not known; but Charles Burney was born in December 1757.

At Lynn, in spite of an execrable instrument, and
an irresponsive audience, the new organist's health
speedily improved. His hearers, if unmusical, were
not unfriendly, and his own good qualities helped him
as of yore. "He scarcely ever entered a house upon
terms of business, without leaving it upon those of
intimacy." He gave music lessons in many of the
great Norfolk mansions,— at Houghton (Lord Orford's),
at Holkham (the home of the Leicesters), at Rainham
(General Lord Townshend's), and at Felbrigge Park
(Mr. Windham's), — padding along the sandy cross-
roads to his destination upon his sure-footed mare
" Peggy," with a certainty that permitted him to study
Tasso or Metastasio in the saddle, and even to consult
a dictionary of his own composing which he carried
in his great-coat pocket. These things, added to correspondence with the Greville circle, projects for a
History of Music, increasing means, and a pleasant
home, made Lynn life very tolerable for a season. But
towards 1759 he seems to have wearied a little of his
provincial lot, added to which, friends began to counsel
his return to town, and to protest against his exile
among "foggy aldermen." "Really, among friends,"
— wrote one of them, to whom we shall often refer
hereafter, — " is not settling at Lynn planting your
youth, genius, hopes, fortune, etc., against a north
wall ? Can you ever expect ripe, high-flavoured fruit,
from such an aspect ? " And then the writer went

on to adjure him to transplant his "spare person," his
"pretty mate," and his "brats" to the more congenial
environment of the capital. He eventually quitted
Lynn in 1760 for London, which he had left about
nine years before.

At this date, he was four and thirty. He set up
his tent in Poland Street, then a rather more favoured
place of residence than it is at present, and having,
beyond the Oxford Road (as Oxford Street was then
called), little but open fields and market gardens.
Portman Square, Manchester Square, Russell Square,
— of all these not a stone had been laid.[1] But Poland
Street was not without aristocratic occupants. The
Duke of Chandos, Sir Willoughby Aston (with whose
daughters the Miss Burneys went to school at Paris),
Lady Augusta Bridges and others were all distinguished neighbours in this now dingy street — to
say nothing of the Cherokee King, who, when he
visited England, actually, to the delight of the
Burney children, took lodgings "almost immediately
opposite." At Poland Street Charles Burney rapidly
became the music master most in request with the
fashionable world. Soon he had not an hour of the
day unoccupied, beginning his rounds as early as
seven in the morning, and finishing them, sometimes,
only at eleven at night. Often he dined in a hackney
coach on the contents of a sandwich box and a flask
of sherry and water. But he must still have found
time for original work, since it was at Poland Street
that, besides "Sonatas for the Harpsichord," he
composed in 1763 the setting for Bonnell Thornton's
Burlesque *Ode on St. Cæcilia's Day*, "adapted to the

[1] *Memoirs of Dr. Burney*, 1832, i. 134.

Antient British Musick; viz.: the Salt Box, the Jew's Harp, the Marrow-Bones and Cleavers, the Hum-Strum or Hurdy-Gurdy," and the rest, which was performed at Ranelagh in masks, to the huge delectation of an audience musical and unmusical, and the amusement of Dr. Johnson.[1] But the pleasures of increasing popularity were dashed by domestic misfortune. Mrs. Burney, the "pretty mate" of the last paragraph, having, in the new home, given birth to a fourth daughter, Charlotte, sickened of consumption. A visit to the Bristol Hot Wells (Clifton) proved unavailing; and to the intense grief of her husband and family, she died, after a brief illness, on the 28th September 1761. She seems to have been a most affectionate mother, and sympathised with her husband in his bookish tastes. With one of his subsequent essays he published a translation from Maupertuis, which she, naturally an excellent French scholar, had executed; and her reading of Pope's *Works* and the *Virgil* of Spence's friend Christopher Pitt, was one of the memories of her daughters. But at the time of her death her eldest child was only twelve, and her youngest a baby.

The little family at Poland Street, thus suddenly

[1] Dr. Birkbeck Hill's Boswell's *Johnson*, 1887, i. 420. In a note communicated by Burney in 1799 to the third edition of Boswell's book, he dates this performance "1769," when (he says) he resided at Norfolk. But his memory must have deceived him, for according to the *Annual Register* for 1763, the Burlesque was performed at Ranelagh on June 10 in that year, having been previously published as a pamphlet, which is to be found in the British Museum; and it figures among the new books for June 1763, in the *Gentleman's Magazine*. The point is a trifling one, only important here because the success of the Ode has been advanced as one of the things which decided its composer to leave Lynn for London in 1760.

left motherless, must have been an exceptionally interesting one. Esther, or Hetty, the eldest, is described as extremely beautiful, and possessed of that fortunate combination, good sense, good humour, and an abundant love of fun. She was besides remarkably musical, and according to the *Gentleman's Magazine*, was wont to astonish her father's guests, at a very early age, by her skilful instrumentalism. James, the eldest son, who, at the age of ten, entered the Navy under Admiral Montagu as a nominal midshipman, was an unusually bright and manly lad, full of vivacity and high spirits. When at school in his Norfolk home, he had been taught by Eugene Aram. He could recall how that "melancholy man" would pace the playground talking of strange deeds to the elder boys ; and he remembered well the memorable night in August 1758 when

> " Two stern-faced men set out from Lynn,
>   Through the cold and heavy mist,
>   And Eugene Aram walk'd between,
>   With gyves upon his wrist." [1]

James Burney rose to eminence in his profession, — sailed twice round the world with Captain Cook, was with him at his death, and lived to be a fine specimen of the old-time sailor, cheery and humorous, unpolished externally, but "gentle and humane" at heart. Charles Lamb loved him; Southey depicts him in his Captainhood as "smoking after supper, and letting out puffs at one corner of his mouth, and puns at the other"; and he dropped Hazlitt out of

---

[1] Admiral Burney's recollections are referred to in Hood's "Preface" to the separate issue of *The Dream of Eugene Aram* published in 1831, with William Harvey's illustrations.

his whist parties, to which he was as attached as
Mrs. Battle, because " W. H." had affronted him by
reviewing his sister Fanny's *Wanderer* severely in
the *Edinburgh*. In this brief biography James Burney
cannot often appear hereafter, which must excuse
these anticipations. The third child, Susanna, or, to
be exact, Susanna Elizabeth, was also remarkable for
her sweetness and charm. Joseph Baretti praised her
dolcissima voce; her knowledge of music was affirmed
to be exact and critical; and her native literary faculty
was as fine, if not as imperative, as that of her sister
Frances. Charles, the second boy, was still in the
nursery; and Charlotte was a baby. Neither of these
last can have had much influence on Frances, who with
Esther, Susanna, and James made up the little group
of clever children which delighted Charles Burney's
friends, from Garrick to the singer Pacchieroti. " All!
all ! very clever girls " (James was of course at sea) —
said this observer later in his queer broken English.
"Sense and *witta* (*sic*) inhabit *here*. . . . All I meet
with at Dr. Burney's house are superior to other people.
I am myself the only *Bestia* that enters the house. I
am, indeed, *a truly* Beast" — by which the poor
gentleman in his humility, as Mrs. Ellis suggests,
obviously intended no more than is conveyed by the
French *bête*.

In the above enumeration of Charles Burney's
children, Frances has been intentionally passed over,
and to Frances we now turn. Like many other
persons destined to make their mark in this world,
she does not seem to have impressed it greatly at the
outset. Neither for beauty nor physique was she
notable in childhood; indeed she was both short and

short-sighted. She was besides extremely shy and silent, as well as backward in most things. At the age of eight she had not learned to read, and her sailor brother used often to divert himself by giving her a book upside down in order to see what she would make of it. Mrs. Burney's friends used to call her the "little dunce"; but her shrewder mother "had no fear of Fanny." For it was observed, by those who looked close, that her perceptive faculties were exceedingly acute; that, in a quiet way, she noticed many things; that she was full of humour and invention in her play; and that whenever she went with the rest to Mrs. Garrick's box at Drury Lane, although she could not read the piece acted, she was quite capable of mimicking the actors, and even of putting appropriate speeches into their mouths. These exhibitions, however, she would only give in the strictest domestic privacy. Before strangers, she became at once the demure, reserved, and almost sheepish little person whom it was the custom to designate familiarly as "the old lady." An anecdote related by her father illustrates some of these peculiarities of character. Next door to the Burneys in Poland Street lived a wig-maker who supplied the voluminous full-bottomed periwigs then favoured by the gentlemen of the Law. The Burney girls used to play with the wig-maker's daughters, and one day the playmates got access to the wig-magazine. They then proceeded to array themselves in what Fanny's later friend Dr. Hawkesworth calls "the honours of the head," dancing about in great delight at their ridiculous figures. Unfortunately one of the ten-guinea flaxen masterpieces soused suddenly into a garden tub filled with water, and forthwith losing all its portentous "Gorgon buckle," was declared by the manufacturer to be totally spoilt. "He was extremely angry," says Fanny's father, "and chid very severely his own children; when my little daughter, the old lady, then ten years of age [1762], advancing to him, as I was informed, with great gravity and composure, sedately says: 'What signifies talking so much about an accident? The wig is wet, to be sure; and the wig was a good wig, to be sure; but it's of no use to speak of it any more; because what's done can't be undone.'"[1] Dr. Johnson himself could not have been more oracular, though he would probably have said (as indeed he does in *Rasselas*) — "What cannot be repaired is not to be regretted!"

At this point it becomes necessary to introduce a personage who, for the future, plays no inconsiderable part in Frances Burney's biography. Mention has been made of a friend by whom Charles Burney was advised to exchange the north wall of Lynn for a more congenial London aspect. This was one Samuel Crisp, a gentleman twenty years older than Fanny's father, who had made his acquaintance when acting as musical companion to Fulke Greville. Samuel Crisp was a person of some importance in his day, — a man of taste and fashion, good-looking, well-mannered and accomplished, having gifts both artistic and musical, — friendly alike with the Duchess of Portland and Mrs. Montagu, — with Lady Coventry and Richard Owen Cambridge, — with Quin and Garrick. Like many of equal abilities, he had dabbled in literature; and two years after Fanny's birth, Garrick

[1] *Memoirs of Dr. Burney*, 1832, ii. 170-1.

had produced at Drury Lane, not without pressure from the writer's aristocratic supporters, a tragedy which Crisp had essayed upon a subject already treated more than a hundred years before by John Webster, — the story of Virginia. Crisp's play cannot be said to have failed, for it ran for two nights more than Johnson's *Irene*. But, on the other hand, it was not a genuine success, although Garrick, besides supplying an excellent Prologue and Epilogue, himself acted Virginius to the Virginia of Mrs. Cibber. The truth is, it was dull, — too dull even to be galvanised into mock vitality by the energy of the manager. No alterations could thenceforth persuade Garrick to revive it, and the author was naturally deeply chagrined. In a frame of mind very unfriendly to humanity in general, he carried his mortification to Italy. Returning in due course somewhat soothed and restored, he settled at Hampton, furnishing a house there so lavishly with guests, pictures, bustos, and musical instruments that he speedily began to exhaust his sources of income. His annoyance at this discovery being aggravated by gout, in a fit of spleen he sold his villa by the Thames; and determining to realise Pope's " the world forgetting, by the world forgot," took sanctuary with a friend in a secluded part of the country.

The retreat he selected was at Chessington, or — as it was then spelled — Chesington Hall, a rambling and ruinous old house between Kingston and Epsom. At this date, though on high ground, it stood in the middle of a wild and almost trackless common, which separated it effectually from the passing stranger. Its owner, Mr. Christopher Hamilton, was an old friend of Crisp and, since the house was too large for his means, only too pleased to welcome as an inmate, a companion who should share his expenses. At Chessington Crisp lived thirty years, and at Chessington he was buried. Until he became too infirm, he quitted it annually for a few weeks every spring, when he repaired to Town to visit his old haunts, look in at a concert or two, and run through the principal picture galleries. Lord Macaulay has described him as "hiding himself like a wild beast in a den," in consequence of the failure of his tragedy, which — as we have seen — was rather indulgently received, at all events on the stage.[1] But Lord Macaulay had not before him all the information we have at present. Although Crisp rated his tragic powers too high, and consequently felt his qualified success more acutely, it is probable that impaired health and reduced means had most to do with his withdrawal to Chessington; and there is no particular evidence that his seclusion, though strict, was savage. In one of his periodical visits to London, he happened upon Burney; came at once to see him at Poland Street; grew keenly interested in his motherless children, and thenceforward continued to be the life-long ally and adviser of the family. Chessington Hall became a haven of rest for the Burneys, — "a place of peace, ease, freedom, and cheerfulness," to which, even when it was later turned into a boarding-house by Miss Hamilton, the father retired to work at his books, and the children for change of air. As Crisp grew older,

---

[1] Crisp's *Virginia* was published anonymously by Tonson in 1754 with a dedication to the writer's friends, the Earl and Countess of Coventry.

they grew more and more necessary to his existence, filling the dark passages and tapestried chambers of the old house with fiddles and harpsichords, dancing, amateur acting, and all the stir and bustle of their fresh and healthy vitality. Their company must have been invaluable to a host, contracted, but by no means wedded, to melancholy; and there is no doubt that in return his experience of the world, his sterling good sense, and his educated taste were of the greatest service to them. They brightened and cheered his life; but they also owed not a little to the personage whom, in brief space, they came to designate affectionately as " Daddy " Crisp.

For two or three years after Mrs. Burney's death not much is known of her husband's doings. His grief at first was intense; but like many sensible men, he at once sought to mitigate it by hard work, attempting among other things a prose translation of Dante's *Inferno*. In June 1764 he paid a short visit to Paris in order to place Hetty and Susan at school there. Fanny was older than Susan, but apart from her general backwardness, her father seems to have apprehended that her very emotional character (she had been overpowered with grief at her mother's death) might, when on the Continent, perhaps induce her to adopt the creed of her grandmother, Mrs. Sleepe, to whom she was much attached. In the French capital, Charles Burney found many friends, and under the influence of Paris air, Paris clothes, Paris festivities and the *Comédie Italienne*, began speedily — like Garrick in the same place a few months afterwards — to recover his spirits, and interest himself once more in his old pursuits. Either now or later, he set to work upon a version of Rousseau's musical *intermède*, the *Devin du Village*, under the title of *The Cunning Man*.[1] Towards the end of June, he left Hetty and Susan in the care of a certain Mme. St. Mart. They remained at Paris for about two years, returning in 1767.

The first diarist of the family appears to have been Susan Burney, who began her records at the early age of ten. Soon after her return home she sketched the portraits of her two elder sisters. "The characteristics of Hetty seem to be wit, generosity, and openness of heart : — Fanny's, — sense, sensibility, and bashfulness, and even a degree of prudery. Her understanding is superior, but her diffidence gives her a bashfulness before company with whom she is not intimate, which is a disadvantage to her. My eldest sister shines in conversation, because, though very modest, she is totally free from any *mauvaise hont :* were Fanny equally so, I am persuaded she would shine no less. I am afraid that my eldest sister is too communicative, and that my sister Fanny is too reserved. They are both charming girls — *des filles comme il y en a peu.*"[2] The words make one think that the composing of *Caractères* or *Portraits* must have formed part of Mme. St. Mart's *curriculum*. At all events they are all we know of Frances Burney at this time, and they coincide with what we have learned already. Doubt-

[1] *The Cunning Man* (*i.e.* fortune-teller or soothsayer) was produced at Drury Lane in 1766 when Rousseau came to England, but it was coldly received (*Biographia Dramatica*, 1812, ii. 145).

[2] In Letter LXIV. of *Evelina*, Miss Burney, applying this locution to Lord Orville, attributes it to Marmontel. The above passage is printed in the "Introduction" to the *Diary and Letters*, 1892, i. pp. xi-xii.

less, during the absence of her sisters in France, she
had been slowly developing. To her busy father, although he left her much to herself, she was devotedly
attached; and she had grown almost as fond of the
adopted parent who had now become her "guide,
philosopher and friend." When Hetty and Susan
were away, she probably saw a great deal of Mr. Crisp,
and in the beginning of 1766 paid her first visit to
the "dear, ever dear Chesington" which was to figure
so frequently in her future journals. It had been her
father's intention that she and her younger sister
Charlotte should also have the advantage of two years'
schooling at Mme. St. Mart's establishment; but the
project, first postponed, was afterwards abandoned in
consequence of Mr. Burney's second marriage.

This took place in October, 1767. The lady, Elizabeth Allen, was the widow of a wealthy Lynn wine-
merchant. She had been the intimate friend of the
late Mrs. Burney, whose death she had deplored
almost as much as Mrs. Burney's husband. She had
three children; but owing to losses in her widowhood,
apparently possessed nothing but a dower-house in
the churchyard of St. Margaret's at Lynn. Coming
to London for the education of her eldest daughter,
Maria, she renewed her acquaintance with the
Burneys. Handsome, intelligent, well-read, and something of a blue-stocking to boot, she seems speedily
to have inspired in Mr. Burney an affection as genuine
as her own for him. But as her Lynn relatives were
not likely to approve the match, seeing particularly
that Mr. Burney had six children of his own, the
marriage took place privately at St. James's, Piccadilly;
and the newly wedded pair, with the connivance of the

friendly Crisp, spent their honeymoon in a farm-house near Chessington. Even then, the matter was kept quiet, being only revealed at last by the misdelivery of a letter. After this, the second Mrs. Burney took her place definitively as the mistress of the Poland Street home, and the Lynn dower-house became an additional holiday resort for the combined family. The children on both sides seem to have been delighted with an alliance which brought them more intimately together; and the new mamma increased rather than diminished the literary tone of the house. "As Mrs. Stephen Allen," says Mrs. Ellis, "she had held a sort of *bas bleu* meeting once a week; as Mrs. Burney, she received men of letters, or art, almost daily, in an informal way." One result of the marriage, as already stated, was that Fanny and Charlotte did not go to Paris. Charlotte was put to school in Norfolk; and it was arranged that Susanna should teach Fanny French.

At the time of her father's second marriage, Fanny Burney was in her sixteenth year. Whether she had written much previous to the return of her sisters from Paris, cannot be affirmed; but it is evident that, with the advent of the diary-keeping Susanna, her native bias to scribbling rapidly increased. Every available scrap of paper was covered with stories and humorous sketches, confided only to the discreet ears of the younger sister, who laughed and cried over these masterpieces in secret. But it so chanced that Mrs. Burney the second, with all her appreciation of the *monde parleur*, was also keenly alive to the *misères du monde scribe*. Something led her to suspect that the girls were writing a good deal more than in her opinion was good for them, and the result was that they were gently but firmly admonished not to spend too much time in idle crude inventions. Thus, one fine day, it came about that, in the paved play-court at Poland Street, when her father was at Chessington and her stepmother at Lynn, the docile Fanny "made over to a bonfire" all her accumulated stock of prose compositions. In the Preface to her last novel of *The Wanderer*, where it is added that Susanna stood weeping by, the date of this holocaust is given as her fifteenth birthday (June 1767). But as it obviously occurred some time after her father's second marriage in October of the same year, her memory must have deceived her. Among the papers she burned was said to be an entire work of fiction, to which we shall return. Luckily, — although by this act she provisionally abjured authorship, and the discredit supposed to attach in the polite world to female writers and female writers of novels and romances in particular, — she did not refrain from journal-keeping. For the date of her first entry in her *Early Diary* is May 30 [1768], at which time Mr. Burney's second marriage had been publicly acknowledged.

Before dealing with those portions of this chronicle which concern the present chapter, it is necessary to say something of the proceedings of the father of the family. In 1769 Mr. Burney, of whom we shall hereafter speak as "Dr." Burney, received his Mus. D. degree at Oxford, his preliminary exercise being an anthem which was performed in the Music School, where it "was received with universal applause."[1] The chief vocalist was one of the Doctor's

[1] *Oxford Journal*, 23 June 1769.

pupils, Miss Jenny Barsanti, often referred to in the *Diary;* and Fanny wrote some congratulatory verses to her father on his distinction, which, at all events, exhibit a knack of rhyming. The receipt of his degree appears to have revived all Dr. Burney's dormant literary ambitions. In matters connected with his profession he had always been an industrious note-taker; and he was also much interested in astronomy. One of the results of this last taste was an anonymous pamphlet prompted by the comet of 1769, at the close of which year it was published. To this was appended the translation from Maupertuis by the first Mrs. Burney, of which mention has been made. The *Essay on Comets* attracted no notice; but it served to strengthen its author's hand; and he began systematically to look over the miscellaneous collections he had accumulated towards that *History of Music* of which he had dreamed at Lynn. In arranging and transcribing the mass of material, Fanny fell naturally into the office of amanuensis and keeper of the records. But these had not long been manipulated before her father discovered that it would be necessary for him to make a personal tour in France and Italy, — first, to procure information in regard to ancient music, and secondly, to ascertain, by ear and eye, the actual condition of the musical art on the Continent. At Paris he visited Rousseau and Diderot, both of whom were interested and helpful. At Ferney he had a chance interview with Voltaire, then seventy-eight and wasted to a skeleton, but still working ten hours a day, and writing without spectacles. Discord, rather than harmony, was the topic of this conversation. The quarrels of authors — Voltaire held — were good for

letters, just as, in a free government, the quarrels of
the great and the clamours of the small were necessary
to liberty.   The silence of critics (he said) did not so
much prove the age to be correct, as dull.   Dr. Burney
had started in June 1770; he did not return until
January 1771, when he almost immediately buried
himself at Chessington to prepare his notes and journal
for the press.   In the following May his book was
printed under the title of *The Present State of Music in
France and Italy; or, the Journal of a Tour through those
Countries, undertaken to collect Materials for a General
History of Music;* and it obtained a considerable success.   Copies went to Mason, Hawkesworth, Garrick,
and Crisp, all of whom had aided in its progress.
Among its other readers must have been Johnson,
who told Mr. Seward that he had "that clever
dog, Burney" in his eye when, two years later, he
wrote his own *Journey to the Western Islands of Scotland.* [1]

During Dr. Burney's absence abroad, his wife
had found the Poland Street house too small.   She
accordingly fixed upon a fresh residence in Queen

[1] Dr. Birkbeck Hill (Boswell's *Johnson*, 1887, iv. 186 n.) seems,
perhaps not unnaturally, to doubt this, as Burney "writes chiefly
of music."   But it is confirmed by a passage in the *Early Diary*,
1889, i. 212.   "He [Baretti] told my father that Dr. Johnson . . .
has read both his Tours with great pleasure, and has pronounced
him to be *one of the first writers of the age* for travels!"   Moreover, in the second Tour, the author was less chary of personal
anecdote.   In Edward FitzGerald's letters, he draws Carlyle's
attention to some of the very interesting particulars which the
second Tour contains concerning Frederick the Great (*More Letters
of Edward FitzGerald*, 1901, p. 67).   But Carlyle, who quotes the
visit to Voltaire from the first Tour, does not mention the second
at all.

Square, Bloomsbury, which was then much more in the country than it is at present. The new home was at the upper end of the square, which had been considerately left open by the architect so as to afford a delightful prospect, across Lamb's Conduit Fields, of Highgate and Hampstead, which Miss Burney — we regret to say — spells "Hygate and Hamstead." There was also a special interest in the house itself, for it had once been inhabited by Queen Anne's printer, Alderman Barber, the "*Johannes Tonsor*" and "very good and old friend" of Swift; and it was a fond tradition of the Burney household that the author of *Gulliver's Travels* had often dined with Barber at Queen Square. But the *Journal to Stella*, when it mentions Barber, invariably refers to him as in the City; and it is probable that Swift visited him uniformly at his place of business. In any case, the Queen Square house was "well fitted up, convenient, and handsome." Especially was there a closet or playroom up two pair of stairs where Fanny could retire to compose her Diary, for which task, during her father's absence abroad, she had unexpected opportunities. But she had also another and more picturesque asylum in her step-mother's dower-house at Lynn. At the end of a long side garden was a "Look Out" or Gazebo, called "The Cabin," from which ships could be seen on the Ouse. Here, except when she was driven from it to the more secluded garden by the profane language of the seafaring population, she was accustomed to write and dream at her ease.

Dr. Burney's activity did not permit him to pause long after his first book. Very soon we hear that he is learning German, — no doubt with a purpose. In July, 1772, he set out upon a second tour, this time to collect materials for his history in Germany and the Netherlands. During his absence, which lasted five months, his family lived mainly at Lynn and Chessington. In December he returned to England, terminating his travels by an unique experience. Upon his passage to Dover, in the very stormy winter of 1772, he was so exhausted by sea-sickness that he fell asleep in his berth, and was carried back again to Calais. On reaching Queen Square he had a severe illness, requiring to be carefully nursed by his family; but, with his customary energy, dictated to his daughters, from his bed, portions of the new Tour whenever the intervals of pain permitted him to do so. As soon as he was convalescent, he hastened off to Chessington, carrying his secretaries with him. The result of his labours was at press in February, 1773, and was published in May. It was received even more kindly than its predecessor, and included detailed *Proposals* for the forthcoming *General History of Music*. Not many months after, in consequence of difficulties as to title, the Queen Square house was given up, and the Burneys moved to Leicester Fields.

With some account of the next new house, which had, even then, its history, we may fitly open a fresh chapter. In closing this one, however, something must be said as to that *Early Diary* which Fanny Burney began to keep in May 1768. When, in 1842–6, her *Diary and Letters* were edited by her sister Charlotte's daughter, Mrs. Charlotte Francis Barrett, an amiable and learned lady who happily combined a knowledge of Hebrew with a genius for making jelly, it was thought right to withhold the portions preceding the publication of *Evelina*, as being " of a more private

and personal nature than that which attaches to the
Journal after its writer became universally known."
But in 1889, this earlier portion also was edited by the
late Mrs. Annie Raine Ellis from the original MSS.
which the first writer, in her own words, had freely
"curtailed and erased of what might be mischievous
from friendly or Family Considerations." One of the
explanatory memoranda states, and another repeats,
that the record was begun at the age of fifteen. Prefixed to the Diary, and "Addressed to a Certain Miss
Nobody," is a whimsical Introduction, which Mrs.
Barrett reproduced in *facsimile* at the beginning of the
Diary and Letters of 1842–6. This, of course, may be
earlier than the rest, as it is said to be on older paper,
and in a slightly different hand. The Diary that
follows, as already stated, was considerably revised by
the writer in her old age; and, as reprinted in 1889,
shows numerous omissions. Of the record for 1769, for
example, Mrs. Ellis says, "Much has been cut from
the Diary of this year, and it has many erasures. It
appears to have been in two or three *cahiers*, which all
lie now within one quarto sheet of paper, so much are
they shrunk in size." There are also large excisions
in the accounts for 1771 and 1772; and the manuscript
everywhere bears token of wholesale obliterations.
Where these are Miss Burney's own, they are said to
be so effectual that scarcely a word can be read. In
future chapters, we shall take leave to make sundry
extracts from the Burney chronicle; but in this, where
only a brief period (1768–73) is in question, we may
fairly confine our citations to a few notes, relating
mainly to the diarist and her method.

In the first lines of her address to Nobody, Miss

Burney defines her purpose. The reason, she says, which induces her to keep a Journal is that, "when the hour arrives in which time is more nimble than memory," she may have some account of her "thoughts, manners, acquaintance and actions." Writing in the Cabin at Lynn a little later, she reverts to this idea. "I cannot express the pleasure I have in writing down my thoughts, at the very moment — my opinion of people when I first see them, and how I alter, or how confirm myself in it — and I am much deceived in my *fore sight*, if I shall not have very great delight in reading this *living proof* of my manner of passing my time, my sentiments, my thoughts of people I know, and a thousand other things in future — there is something to me very unsatisfactory in passing year after year, without even a memorandum of what you did, etc." Presently, she has her difficulties. Dr. Burney comes upon a fugitive page of this *chronique intime*, and though he does not forbid the practice, protests that if he finds it lying about he will post it up in the market place. Then one of her mother's friends, Miss Dorothy Young (whom the first Mrs. Burney on her death-bed had recommended her husband to marry) had her doubts about this "most dangerous employment." "Suppose now," says Miss Young, "your favourite wish were granted, and you were *to fall in love* [it may be noted that Fanny had already confided this tender aspiration to her pages], and then the object of your passion were to get sight of some part which related to himself?" Here was an appalling suggestion, to which Fanny could only reply that she should have to take a precipitate trip to Rosamond's Pond in St. James's Park, then the last resort of the despairing.

It is characteristic of this very early entry in the Diary, that the conversation is given exactly as if it had been reported in shorthand. As the record progresses, there are many similar instances of this practice, which greatly irritated distrustful Mr. Croker. "I shall recollect as much of the conversation as I can, and make the parties speak for themselves," Miss Burney writes of a long interview with the currish misogynist and Tory, Dr. John Shebbeare. And then follows a dialogue to which the names of the speakers are prefixed as they would be in a play.

Some of the most interesting entries at this date relate to her reading, and show that, instead of being, as Lord Macaulay supposed,[1] an infrequent student of novels, her activity in this way was fully equal to her opportunities. Richardson's works she must have known intimately, as she reminds her sister of their early love for him; she reads and cries over and criticises the *Vicar of Wakefield;* she reads *Rasselas,* and thinks the style and sentiments inimitable. The subject however is dreadful. " How terrible is it to be told by a man of his [Johnson's] genius and knowledge, in so affectingly probable a manner, that true, real happiness is ever unattainable in this world ! " The *Sentimental Journey,* which was a special favourite with her step-mother, she read three times; and, from a reference to " Hobby Horses," was probably acquainted with *Tristram Shandy,* or at all events

---

[1] Lord Macaulay relied upon the fact, mentioned in the Dedication to *The Wanderer* (p. xxii), that Dr. Burney's large library only contained one novel, Fielding's *Amelia.* But, as Mrs. Ellis pertinently remarks, " Novels were brought into the house if they did not abide in it."

with its famous eighth chapter. Stranger still, she had
not only read Prévost's *Doyen de Killérine* (with which
she is delighted), but that very stimulating work, the
Vie de Marianne of Marivaux. Further, she occasionally quotes much inferior productions, *e.g.* the
Henry and Frances of Mrs. Griffiths, the *Lady Julia
Mandeville* of the once popular Mrs. Brooke, and the
Lydia of Shebbeare. These are advanced mainly in
answer to Lord Macaulay. But the *Diary* contains
numerous references to studies of a sterner sort.
Among the books she speaks of reading, are Plutarch's
Lives, Pope's *Iliad* and *Odyssey*, Hawkesworth's *Tele-
machus*, Hume, Smollett, Smith's *Thucydides*, Middle-
ton's *Cicero*, Hooke's *Roman*, and Stanyan's *Grecian
History*, — all of which she professes to go through
systematically. Here is strong meat enough, one
would imagine, for a budding Mme. Roland; — certainly it would be a trying course, in the days when skip-
ping was unknown, for even that model and methodical
student, Miss Clarissa Harlowe. Moreover it proves
plainly that Fanny's close attention to braid-stitch,
cross-and-change, pinking, pointing, frilling, and all
the other niceties of that needlework which her step-
mother regarded as so important to young persons —
did not leave her without leisure for literature.

To give any detailed summary of the material contained in the first four years of Miss Burney's *Diary*
would be impracticable here. There are several portraits which (like that of Dr. Shebbeare) show that
the writer's pen is already working willingly and
easily in what was to be her most congenial field.
There is a long description of the forgotten Spanish
traveller, Mr. Richard Twiss, a polyglot eccentric of

the first water; there is another of a delightful fop and cousin, Richard Burney, of Worcester, Junr., the son of Dr. Burney's elder brother; there is a picturesque *Journal*, addressed to Susan in 1773, of a visit to Teignmouth, — or "Tingmouth," as the writer calls it, — which Mrs. Ellis fairly characterises as "Fanny's first book, privately circulated," and which contains some lively sketches of rural sports and watering-place oddities. Some of these descriptions and portraits go off in letters to "Daddy" Crisp at Chessington, who is delighted, and gives his "dearest Fannikin" some very seasonable advice, which, in after years, she unhappily neglected. "If once you set about framing studied letters, that are to be correct, nicely grammatical, and run in smooth periods, I shall mind them no otherwise than as newspapers of intelligence. . . . There is no fault in an epistolary correspondence like stiffness and study. Dash away whatever comes uppermost; the sudden sallies of imagination, clap'd down on paper, just as they arise, are worth folios. . . . Never think of being correct when you write to me." Not the least notable of Fanny's records are the glimpses we get of some of her father's friends. One is poor mad Kit Smart, always needy and out-at-elbows, with whom Burney had grown acquainted at Arne's, and who died in 1772 in the King's Bench Prison. Another, who also died in this period, is Hawkesworth, whose end, according to Fanny, was certainly hastened by the attacks made upon him in connection with his subsidised publication of Cook's *Voyages*. Garrick more or less pervades the chronicle, dashing into the house in the most unexpected manner; rushing away with little Charlotte

whom he declares to be the image of *Comedy* in
Reynolds's picture; acting, grimacing, mimicking,
posturing, and altogether comporting himself in every
respect like the excellent friend and histrion he was.
Fanny often sees him play—as Bayes in the *Rehearsal;*
as Richard the Third; as Lear, and as Abel Drugger
in the *Alchemist.* Of "crook'd back'd Richard" she
says,—"It is inconceivable how terribly great he is in
this character! I will never see him so disfigured
again; he seemed so truly the monster he performed,
that I felt myself glow with indignation every time
I saw him. The applause he met with, exceeds all
belief in the absent. I thought at the end they would
have torn the house down: our seats shook under us."
Of Lear,—"He was exquisitely great; every idea I
had formed of his talents, although I have ever idolised
him, was exceeded." But she very properly blames
Cibber's feeble alterations of Shakespeare's work. As
to Abel Drugger, perhaps Garrick's greatest part, she
says:—"Never could I have imagined such a meta-
morphose as I saw; the extreme meanness, the
vulgarity, the low wit, the vacancy of countenance, the
appearance of *unlicked nature* in all his motions."
These are more than the opinions of an "unlessoned
girl," for they are confirmed to the full by experienced
spectators such as Lichtenberg and Mme. Necker. To
Goldsmith, then not far from his end, there is passing
reference. "Dr. Goldsmith"—says the diary in May,
1773—"has just brought on the stage a new comedy,
called, 'She stoops to *Conquer.*' We went to it with
Mr. and Mrs. Young; it is very laughable and comic;
but I know not how it is, almost all diversions are
insipid at present to me, except the opera." There is

another mention of Goldsmith a few pages further on. It relates to his projected *Dictionary of Arts and Sciences*. Among other contributors, Dr. Burney was to undertake the article " Musician." But the plan never got beyond the prospectus stage. Goldsmith died in the following year, and Dr. Burney's paper probably found its ultimate place in his own *History of Music*.

CHAPTER II

No. 1, St. Martin's Street, now No. 35, to which the
Burneys moved early in 1774, may fairly be described
as a house with a history. We say "now," since it
still exists, — standing to the right at the top of the
little street which opens into Leicester Square from the
south; and having on its left that Orange Street Con-
gregational Church where, in its Huguenot days, was
wont to preach Wesley's opponent, — the Rev. Augustus
Montague Toplady. The house itself, once red brick,
but at present stuccoed over, is not impressive, save
for the distinction conferred by a Society of Arts tablet
which proclaims it to have been formerly the residence
of Newton. Miss Burney, indeed, as her father supposed, declares that Sir Isaac built it; but this is an
error. He took it in 1710, when he was nearing
seventy, and he lived in it until 1725, two years before
he died at Kensington. Beyond occasional visits to
the Princess Caroline at Leicester House on the
opposite side of the Fields; and the fact that he
superintended the production of two editions of the
Principia during his period of residence, no very
definite traditions belong to his sojourn in St. Martin's
Street. But Dr. Burney, who valued literary associa-

31

tion, had a better reason for connecting his new
house with Swift, than he had for connecting him
with Queen Square. For in Newton's house in
St. Martin's Street had certainly dwelt one of Swift's
intimates and Newton's relatives, the beautiful and
witty Catherine Barton, — the "*jolie nièce*" of Voltaire,
— and the "Super-intendant of his domestick Affairs"
to Charles Montagu, Earl of Halifax, to whom, it is
conjectured, she was privately married. After the
death of Halifax in 1715, she became the wife of
John Conduitt, Newton's successor as Master of
the Mint; and, when in town, was accustomed to
reside with her uncle in Leicester Fields. And it is
no great stretch of imagination to assume that, at such
times, though Swift himself was in exile, she was
visited by the other old friends who had clustered
around her when she was a Toast of the Kit Cats.
The chairs of Lady Worsley and Lady Betty Ger-
maine must often have waited at the narrow approach by which the street was then entered from
the Fields, while their mistresses "disputed Whig and
Tory" with Mrs. Conduitt, or were interrupted in a
tête-à-tête by Gay and the Duchess of Queensberry.[1]

As regards situation, the change from Queen Square
to St. Martin's Street was not entirely for the better.
It was no small loss to substitute an "unpleasant site,"
"confined air," and a "shabby immediate neighbourhood" for the unobstructed view of "Hampstead's

[1] Catherine Hyde was still living in Fanny Burney's day;
and Fanny saw her at Covent Garden Theatre in January 1773,
when Mason's *Elfrida* was being acted. "I had the pleasure to
see Prior's celebrated fair 'Kitty, beautiful and young,' now called
Kitty, *beautiful and old*, in the stage box." (*Early Diary*, 1889,
i. p. 184.)

breezy Heath" which the Bloomsbury home afforded.[1]
But in the way of convenience, and a central position,
the difference was great, in addition to which, compared
with its predecessor, the new residence was "large and
good." It is true that the stairs were so steep and
narrow that one of Fulke Greville's friends broke his
sword in climbing them ; but, on the other hand, most
of the rooms were panelled, and one, at least, of the
ceilings "prodigiously painted and ornamented," not,
as the Doctor was careful to explain, by him, but by
previous occupants. The chief glory of the house,
however, was the unpretentious structure at the top,
which passed for Sir Isaac's observatory. It is perhaps
safest to say "passed," because, between 1725 and
1774, there must have been other dwellers in No. 1, St.
Martin's Street, and many things may have happened.
But the Burneys seem to have devoutly believed in the
small-paned, wooden turret, with the leaden roof and
tiny fireplace, which embodied so respectable a tradition. They exhibited it religiously to their visitors ;
and one of its new owner's first acts was to put it into
repair. When, four years later, it was all but whirled
away by the hurricane of 1778, he practically rebuilt
it. And it was unquestionably Fanny's chosen retreat
and *scriptorium*. "His [Newton's] observatory is my
favourite sitting place, where I can retire to read or
write any of my private fancies or vagaries." And
then follows what — having regard to some of her previous utterances — is more interesting than unexpected.[2]

[1] "There are now," said Cunningham, writing as far back as
1849, "at least 2 square miles of brick and mortar between it
[Queen Square] and the view." (*Handbook for London*, ii. p. 686.)

[2] See *ante*, p. 19.

D

" I burnt all up to my fifteenth year—thinking I grew
too old for scribbling nonsense, but as I am less young,
I grow, I fear, less wise, for I cannot any longer resist
what I find to be irresistible, the pleasure of popping
down my thoughts from time to time upon paper."

Whatever may have been her exact age at the date
of the famous *auto-da-fé* in the paved court at Poland
Street, she must have been nearing two and twenty
when she "popped down" the foregoing passage; and
the moment, taken in connection with the change of
scene from Bloomsbury to Leicester Fields, is a favourable one for reviewing the Burney family circle in
1774–5. Dr. Burney's second or German Tour, as we
know, had been published in 1773; and in the same
year he had been made a Fellow of the Royal Society.
At present, in the intervals of rheumatism, he was
working, with Fanny's aid, at his *History of Music*. By
his second wife he had two children,— Richard, and
Sarah Harriet, the latter of whom eventually, like her
gifted half-sister, became a novelist. But both Richard
and Harriet, at this date, were in the nursery. Esther,
or Hetty, the eldest daughter, had been married for
some time to her cousin, Charles Rousseau Burney,
afterwards of Bath, a musician and former pupil of
her father; while Maria Allen, the daughter of Dr.
Burney's second wife, was married to a Mr. Rishton.
James Burney, the sailor, having sailed with Cook
in his second voyage, and been made a lieutenant,
had now returned home. In 1775 he was serving on
the North American Station, when he was recalled to
accompany Cook on his third and fatal expedition. Of
the rest, Susan and Charlotte were now grown up,
Charlotte being about fifteen, and Susan some years

older. Charles, after having enjoyed the reputation
of being "the sweetest-tempered boy in the Charter-
house School," was now, in all probability, pursuing at
Cambridge those studies for which he was eventually
to be classed with Porson and Parr. The only one of
the Queen Square frequenters no longer to be encoun-
tered at St. Martin's Street was "Daddy" Crisp. By
this date he was sixty-eight, and his fits of gout had
become so severe, that he had ceased to make his annual descents upon London from his Surrey hermitage.
But his interest in all that befel his friends at Leicester
Fields remained unabated; and in this he was kept
carefully posted up by his favourite "Fannikin," who,
what with acting as librarian and amanuensis to her
indefatigable father, writing periodical news-letters of
"from six to twelve large quarto pages" to Chessington, and keeping her own voluminous journal besides
— must have been very actively employed both in the
Observatory and out of it.   Not without reason can it
have been that she acquired the "murtherous stooping"
which her Mentor deplored, nor was it entirely charge-
able to the shortness of sight which she shared with
Charlotte Brontë.   It is from her bright and graphic
despatches to Mr. Crisp that we propose to draw most
of the material for this chapter.   Often these are repeated in her *Diary*, and they are also expanded in the
Memoirs of Dr. Burney which she wrote in later years;
but they are at their best and freshest in her letters, —
letters which, in many cases, must have been scribbled
off immediately after the occurrence of the events they
described.   From one of them it is clear that their
writer thought nothing of setting to work at what
would now be considered a very lengthy epistle, when

the entertainment of the evening had come to an end.

The Queen Square circle had already been sufficiently diversified; but it grew wider and even more varied at Leicester Fields. Some of the Doctor's friends were now in his immediate vicinity. The family of Mr. (afterwards Sir Robert) Strange, the engraver, — old Paris acquaintances, — were, for the moment, lodging close by. Reynolds, who had just painted the beautiful Eliza Linley (Mrs. Sheridan) as "St. Cecilia," lived only just across the Fields at No. 47; and Garrick, in the new house recently built for him by the brothers Adam at the Adelphi, was not too far off to be a frequent looker-in. Another artistic friend was the sculptor, Joseph Nollekens, whom Burney had met in Italy. James Barry, the eccentric and pugnacious Irish painter from Castle Street, then engaged in decorating the Council Room of the Society of Arts with vast designs (in one of which Dr. Burney, in a queue and tye-wig, figures incongruously among the nymphs of the Thames), — was also among the familiar faces. But the majority were naturally persons who were more or less attracted to the Historian of Music. In this category comes James Harris of Salisbury, "a most charming old man," — says Fanny, not only the author of *Hermes*, but a writer upon Music, and a composer whose pastoral of *Daphnis and Amaryllis* had actually been produced at Drury Lane. With him was his wife, the delightful Mrs. Harris whose gossiping letters to her son, the first Earl of Malmesbury, are some of the most charming in their kind. Then there was another new friend, whom the Burney girls grew to love almost as much as "Daddy" Crisp himself, the Rev. Thomas Twining of Fordham, near Colchester, afterwards the translator of Aristotle's *Treatise on Poetry*. His acquaintance with Dr. Burney had begun over the *German Tour*, for Twining, too, had meditated a *History of Music*, which he abandoned in favour of Burney's. "They were far from young when they met,"— says Twining's brother and biographer referring to the new friends,— "and they could ill afford to lose time."[1] Besides these, there were the foreign professionals who regarded the author of the *Tours* as the supreme arbiter in matters musical: — the celebrated *soprano*, Lucrezia Agujari, otherwise the *Bastardini;* the almost equally celebrated Caterina Gabrielli, and the *Inglesina*, Cecilia Davies; while the men were represented by the singer and composer, Rauzzini, who is so much commended in the *German Tour*, by Gasparo Pacchieroti and others. Finally, there were the "*Lyons*,"— as the diarist calls them,— the Otaheitan Omai, who had come from the Society Islands with Lieutenant Burney; and the Abyssinian traveller, James Bruce of Kinnaird; and last, but by no means largest, for Bruce was six feet four, the Russian "man-mountain," Alexis Orloff, who had certainly helped to strangle his Imperial Master Peter III., and was also—though not so surely—the reputed favourite of that terrible Czarina who, according to Walpole, had even more teeth than the famous Wild Beast of the Gévaudan. The goings and comings of these, and other notables and notorieties,— for those mentioned

---

[1] In *Recreations and Studies of a Country Clergyman of the Eighteenth Century* [Thomas Twining], 1882, there are several letters from Twining to Burney and *vice versa*, some of which will be hereafter cited.

by no means exhaust the list, — must have been an unexampled school of character to a budding novelist, whose gift lay especially in seizing upon the peculiarities of human nature, whose perceptions were at their freshest and keenest, and whose singularly retentive memory was not yet perplexed and bewildered by too prolonged an experience of the very variegated patchwork of Eighteenth Century society.

Among the first visits to St. Martin's Street that Fanny chronicles is one from that "most entertaining of mortals, Mr. Garrick." He arrived, as usual, very early in the morning, marching straight into the study where Dr. Burney, "surrounded by books and papers innumerable," was having his hair dressed. Fanny was making breakfast; Charlotte reading the paper. Nobody else was a-stir. "My father," — says Miss Burney, — "was beginning a laughing sort of apology for his litters, and so forth, but Mr. Garrick interrupted him with 'Aye now; do be in a little confusion; it will make things comfortable!'" He then began to look gravely at the hairdresser. (Dr. Burney, it may be stated in parenthesis, wore his own hair, — a crop so bushy and luxuriant that Frances Reynolds persisted in regarding it as artificial.) "He (Garrick) was himself in a most odious scratch-wig, which nobody but himself could dare to be seen in. He put on a look in the Abel Drugger style of *envy* and sadness, as he examined the hairdresser's progress; and, when he had done, he turned to him with a dejected face, and said, 'Pray, Sir, could you touch up *this* a little?' taking hold of his own frightful scratch." At which the hairdresser only grinned, and left the room. But Garrick continued his proceedings in the same mirthful spirit.

He made enquiries as to the progress of the *History of
Music*, protesting that he was only waiting to blow the
trumpet of Fame, which he forthwith proceeded to do
with a stick, after the fashion of a Raree-Show-man.
"Here is the only true History, Gentlemen; please to
buy, please to buy. Sir, I shall blow it in the very
ear of yon scurvy magistrate" — by whom he meant
Sir John Hawkins of Twickenham, whom Horace
Walpole had incited to a rival performance. His final
exploit, after mimicking the Spanish traveller, Twiss,
and Dr. Arne, Burney's old master, was to give a
dramatic rendering of an interview he had recently
had with Johnson, — not yet personally known to
the young ladies. Johnson had asked Garrick to
lend him a book, and Johnson's carelessness about
books was notorious. "'David, will you lend me
Petra[r]ca?' 'Yes, Sir.' 'David, you sigh.' 'Sir,
you shall have it.' Accordingly, the book, finely bound,
was sent, but scarce had he received it, when uttering
a Latin ejaculation (which Mr. Garrick repeated) in a
fit of enthusiasm, — over his head goes poor Petra[r]ca,
— Russia leather and all!"[1] After this the mercurial actor bustled off to give breakfast to Boswell,

[1] "So much of his [Garrick's] drollery belongs to his voice,
looks, and manners," says the Diary, "that *writing* loses it
almost all." Yet more than forty years afterwards, in her
Memoirs of her father (1832, i. pp. 352–3), she expanded the
above, about seven lines in the original, to a page and three
quarters. It is clear that she worked from the *Diary*, for
some of the expressions are identical. But many decorative
particulars are added to the record of Garrick's visit, which
are not in the first account. We have preferred the earlier, if
less picturesque, narrative. Boswell, of course, has nothing of
this anecdote ; which was not printed until long after his
death.

promising to come soon and plague them again. By
the Burney household Garrick was idolised; but Miss
Burney hints that where he was not on cordial terms,
he could contrive to make himself extremely disagreeable.

Other early visitors were Bruce, the already mentioned Abyssinian traveller, and the Otaheitan Omai.
We will take the traveller first. At this time he had
been twelve years abroad, four of which had been spent
in unexplored parts of Africa. "His figure is almost
gigantic! he is the tallest man I ever saw," writes
Fanny, — who adds elsewhere that he almost fright-
ened Mr. Twining. "I cannot say I was charmed with
him; for he seems rather arrogant, and to have so large
a share of good opinion of himself, as to have nothing
left for the rest of the world but contempt. Yet his
self-approbation is not that of a *fop;* on the contrary,
he is a very manly character, and looks so dauntless
and intrepid, so that I believe he could never in his
life know what fear meant." Despite his hauteur,
Bruce seems to have taken to the Burneys. He liked
music, and he lodged in Leicester Fields, so he came
often to their social evenings. He even favoured the
Doctor with two drawings, a Theban harp and an
Abyssinian lyre, which were copied for the *History of
Music.* The latter instrument prompted some rather
obvious gibes about Abyssinian *liars* from Walpole and
Selwyn. Bruce, as Johnson said, was "not a distinct
relater," added to which his large, imperious, and rather
swaggering manner prejudiced people against his stories, and had the effect of delaying his account of his ex-
ploits until a few years before his death in 1794. One
of his last appearances at St. Martin's Street was in

1776, when he stayed to supper " which, you know, with us, is nothing but a permission to sit over a table for chat, and roast potatoes, or apples." But "his Abyssinian Majesty," as Fanny calls him, neither discoursed on this occasion upon the Abyssinian lyre, nor the merits of raw beef-steaks as a diet. He only told a long and rather stupid story of a practical joke at a masquerade.

Omiah, Omai, Omy, or familiarly, Jack,— the other " *lyon* of *lyons*," — came to St. Martin's Street upon the invitation of James Burney, whose sister gives detailed accounts of his visits. At the time of the first, the Society Islander, of whom, in his native state, there is a portrait in Cook's *Voyages*, can only have been a few months in England. But although he had not learned English, he had already acquired all the externals of a fine gentleman. He arrived betimes, after a preliminary note in due form, arrayed splendidly in a Court suit of Manchester velvet lined with white satin, a bag, laced ruffles (on his tattooed hands), and a very handsome sword which had been given him by King George the Third. Though not handsome, he was tall and well proportioned. " He makes *remarkable* good bows —not for *him* but for *anybody*, however long under a Dancing Master's care," writes Miss Burney. " Indeed he seems to shame Education, for his manners are so extremely graceful, and he is so polite, attentive, and easy, that you would have thought he came from some Foreign Court," — a sentiment which seems later to have prompted a comparison between the lamentable failure of Lord Chesterfield's precepts to make of Philip Stanhope anything but a " pedantic booby," and the exemplary rapidity with which Otaheitan Omiah had contrived to " cultivate the Graces." Miss Burney saw

Omiah again before he returned to Ulietea. Upon this occasion, he obliged the company with "a song of his own country," which, from his subsequent analysis, must have comprised the entire *scenario* of a comic opera. But his audience were too musical, and it was not a success. "So queer, wild, strange a *rumbling of sounds* never did I before hear, and very contentedly can I go to the grave, if I never do again. His [Omiah's] *song* is the only thing that is *savage* about him." [1]

But it is time — looking to the limitations of our space — to turn from the specific to the general, and give some account of the St. Martin's Street musical evenings. Already at Poland Street and Queen Square these entertainments had been the rule; and at Newton's house, with the Doctor's increasing popularity, they attained their greatest importance. Moreover, they found, as they had not before found, their faithful chronicler in Daddy Crisp's correspondent. The chief performers on ordinary occasions seem to have been Esther Burney and her husband, their *pièce de résistance* being Müthel's Duet for two harpsichords. Another famous harpsichord player was the Baroness Deiden, the wife of the Danish Ambassador, whose reputation is said to have been European. But the "peacock's brains" of the record was certainly the Agujari, and Miss Burney's enthusiasm overflows.

[1] The fate of Cowper's "gentle savage" was pathetic. Painted by Reynolds and patronised by Lord Sandwich,— lionised by Lady Townshend and the Duchess of Devonshire, — he was suffered to go back once more to his own people, among whom he had neither status nor importance. He died soon after, having shown himself (says Vancouver) both "vain and silly." And no wonder !

Carestini, Farinelli, Senesino, all Mr. Crisp's old idols,
— 'twas to these only that the *Bastardini* could be compared. And she seems certainly to have done her best.
She arrived for tea before seven, stayed till twelve,
sang almost all the time, permitted her hearers to
encore nearly every song, and sang moreover in twenty
different styles, minuets, cantabiles, church-music,
bravuras and even that popular Vauxhall *misère*, the
rondeau, growing at last so excited over an *aria parlante* from the *Didone Abbandonata* ("*Son Regina, e sono
Amante*") that "she acted it throughout with great
spirit and feeling." This was pretty well for the lady
whom Macaulay qualifies as the "rapacious" Agujari,
apparently because, at this date, she was earning fifty
pounds a song — which she thoroughly deserved, since
people went to hear her and no one else — at the
Oxford Street Pantheon.[1] But she had an exceedingly
appreciative audience, limited by her own request to
the Burney family; she was tired of singing at concerts, book in hand, "*comme une petite écolière*," and
most of all, she was anxious to give the Historian of
Music, who was also all-powerful in matters operatic,
a taste of her real quality. It does not appear that
she ever repeated her performances at St. Martin's
Street, so that it would be inaccurate to represent her
as figuring habitually and gratuitously at the Burney
"conversations."

One of the next things which Fanny recounts to
Mr. Crisp is the production, at the Opera House in

---

[1] Agujari, according to Grove's *Dictionary of Music*, was the
highest and most extended soprano on record. Her voice
reached "from the middle of the harpsichord to two notes
above it," says Miss Burney.

the Haymarket, of that very *Didone* of Metastasio from which Agujari had borrowed her *aria parlante*. But the *diva* upon this occasion (Saturday, Nov. 11, 1775) was Caterina Gabrielli, who seems to have behaved with all her traditional caprice. The Burney family, who occupied the front row of the first gallery, are terribly divided as to her merits. "She was most *impertinently* easy," says Fanny, "visibly took no pains, and never in the least exerted herself." Elsewhere she writes, "Her voice is feeble, but sweetly toned. She has great powers of execution; but—she is no Agujari!" And thereupon, in the contest and confusion of opinion, the writer turns to a little concert that has just taken place in St. Martin's Street, "at which *assisted* a most superb party of company." It originated in the desire of Dr. King, sometime chaplain to the British factory at St. Petersburg, that the famous Prince Orloff,[1] before he left England, should hear Hetty and her husband in Müthel's duet. Both in her *Diary* and Letters, Fanny has treated this exceptional entertainment at considerable length; and she subsequently "embroidered" the record in the Memoirs of her father. We shall depend, by preference, upon her account to Mr. Crisp. After introducing the guests as they arrive:—Dr. Ogle, the musical Dean of Winchester; Dr. King, who announces consequentially that the Prince, having dined at Lord Buckingham's, is coming as soon as he has been to Lady Harrington's rout; the *virtuosa*, Lady Edgecumbe ("all condescension, *repartee* (*and yet*) good humour"); Mr. Charles Boone, the fine gentleman who broke his sword in the

---

[1] He is generally called "Count." But in her letters, diary, and *Memoirs*, Fanny styles him "Prince."

staircase; Mrs. Brudenel; Mr. Anthony Chamier — all of whose conversation turns upon the Gabrielli and her performance of the evening before, — one of the *rat, tat, tats* with which the diarist diversifies her narrative, announces M. le Baron de Demidoff, thin, long-nosed, with a most *triste* and foreign countenance. M. de Demidoff travels with the Prince, whose *avant-coureur* he is. He brings the gratifying intelligence that His Highness is detained at Lady Harrington's, but may be expected with the least possible delay. Then follow Mr. Harris of Salisbury, Lord Bruce, a younger brother of the Duke of Montague (who has been to St. Martin's *Lane* by mistake) — and so forth. At last — like Charlemagne after his Paladins — appears Prince Orloff, accompanied by General Bawr, a Hessian, stern, martial, who has seen service in the Turkish war. And here we most willingly surrender the pen to Miss Burney. " The Prince is another Mr. Bruce, being immensely tall and stout in pro-portion. He is a handsome and magnificent figure. His dress was very superb. Besides a blue Garter he had a star of diamonds of prodigious brilliancy; he had likewise a *shoulder knot* of the same *precious jewels*, and a picture of the Empress hung from his neck, which was set round with diamonds of such magnitude and lustre that, when near the candle, they were too dazzling for the eye. His jewels, Dr. King says, are valued at above £100,000. He was extremely gracious and polite, and appears to be *addicted to pleasantry*. He speaks very little English but knows French perfectly. He was received by my father in the drawing-room. The library, where the music was, was so crowded, he only shewed himself at the door, where

he bowed to Mr. Chamier, who had met with him
elsewhere."

The Müthel duet, which had been postponed for
the Prince's arrival, was then played with prodigious
applause, relaxing even the "sorrowful countenance"
of the Baron de Demidoff, who clapped his snuff box
rapturously, calling out in broken English, " *Dis is so
pretty as ever I heard in my life!* " Lord Bruce, turning
to Prince Orloff, told him the performers were man
and wife. His Highness seemed surprised, and walking up to Mrs. Burney, made her many compliments;
and, expressing his wonder that two such executants
should chance to be united, added " *Mais, qu'a produit
tant d'Harmonie?* " To this Hetty, in a flutter, could
find no fitter reply than " *Rien Monseigneur, que trois
enfants,*" — that being the extent of her family, —
an artless and unexpected answer at which Monseigneur laughs immoderately, and, being "addicted
to pleasantry," retails freely to those about him, with
many "droll comments and observations" on Mrs.
Burney's words. "When the room was a good deal
thinned" — Fanny goes on — "Mr. Harris told me he
wished some of *the ladies* would express a desire of
seeing the *Empress's picture* nearer. 'I, you know,'
said he, 'as a *man*, cannot, but my old eyes can't see
it at a distance.'" [The truth was, Mr. Harris wished
to be able to compare Orloff's picture of Catherine II.
with his son James's (Lord Malmesbury's) portrait of
the King of Spain.] "I went up to Dr. King, and
made the request to him. He hesitated some time,
but afterwards *hinted* the demand to General Bawr,
who boldly made it to the Prince. His Highness
laughed, and with great good humour desired the

General to untie the picture from his neck, and present it to us; and he was very facetious upon the occasion, desiring to know if we wanted anything else? and saying that if they pleased, *the ladies* might *strip him entirely!* Not very elegant, methinks, his pleasantry! When we got it there was hardly any looking at the Empress for the glare of the diamonds. Their size is almost incredible. One of them, I am sure, was as big as a *nut-meg* at *least*. When we were all satisfied it was returned, and the Prince most graciously made a bow to, and received a curtsie from, everyone who looked at it." [1]

In the remainder of Fanny's letters to Mr. Crisp, she gives an account of a further concert arising out of the famous duet. This time the principal guest was the Count (afterwards the Duke) de Guines, the French Ambassador, who was not only a *virtuoso* of the first order, but an accomplished flute-player, who had the reputation of having dared to beard that other distinguished performer on the same instrument, Frederick the Great. His Majesty had said to him impatiently and impertinently — "*Je vous prie, qu'est-ce que fait votre maître quand il ne peut pas chasser De Guisnes?*" The Count — a typical aristocrat of the pre-Revolution days — shrugged his shoulders, and made answer, "*Il est vrai, Sire, que mon maître n'a pas le bonheur de savoir jouer de la flûte,*" [2] a retort more dexterous than deserved, since Frederick, whom Dr. Burney had listened to at Potsdam, was not by any means a mere amateur. Lady Edgecumbe had talked so much to M. de Guines about the duet, that he expressed a great desire to

---

[1] *Early Diary*, 1889, ii. 121.
[2] *Memoirs of the Margravine of Anspach*, 1826, ii. 125.

hear it, and a second concert had to be arranged.
The company convened on this occasion included Lord
Ashburnham, "Groom of the Stole, and First Lord
of the Bedchamber," the Baron and Baroness Deiden,
Lord Barrington, Lord Sandwich ("Jemmy Twitcher,"
to wit), and Signor Venanzio Rauzzini, the "pius
Æneas" to the Dido of Gabrielli. Rauzzini was
vainly implored to indulge the company with a
Rondeau de sa façon—*i.e.* from his own *Piramo e Tisbe;*
but he pleaded the professional cold. Fanny is
enchanted with the young Roman's appearance. "He
looked like an angel," she writes. "Nothing can be
more beautiful than this youth. He has the com-
plection of our Dick,—the very finest white and red
I ever saw: his eyes are the sweetest in the world,
at once soft and spirited: all his features are animated
and *charming*." "'*Avez vous une Assemblée chez vous
tous les Dimanches,*'[1] cried he, to my father. '*Je
viendrai une autre fois quand je pourrai chanter!*' Only
think how we were *let down! '*Une autre fois!*' cried
Hetty; '*Une autre fois!*' echoed Susette; '*Une autre
fois!*' still more pathetically echoed your humble
servant." But he contributed his quota to the gossip
about the Gabrielli; and when the oft-told story was
repeated as to the extraordinary ceremonial parade
she observed in quitting the Opera House on Satur-

[1] Dr. Burney evidently had mild qualms about these Sunday
concerts. When after the first occasion here referred to, Dr.
King and Dr. Ogle supped at St. Martin's Street, he said that
he hoped for *absolution* from them if there was any crime
in having *music on a Sunday*. To which Dr. Ogle replied
discreetly that music was an excellent thing *any and every
day;* and Dr. King evasively — "Have we not music at
church?"

days, with first a running footman to clear the way, then her sister, then herself, then a page for her train, then another footman, and then a man out of livery to carry her lap-dog in her muff, — Rauzzini interjected, " *Et puis, une autre pour un singe, et un autre pour un perroquet !* " As to "Mrs. Gabrielle" (for so she styled herself on her Golden Square doorplate), it is manifest that her reputation for whim had created considerable prejudice against her. But in the *History of Music* Dr. Burney, who knew her intimately, is much milder in his expressions than the more excitable members of his family. He says that despite her low origin (she was the daughter of a Cardinal's cook at Rome), she had extraordinary grace and dignity of gesture. She was, moreover, he declared, the most intelligent and best-bred *virtuosa* with whom he ever conversed, speaking like a well-educated woman, who had seen the world, not only on music, but on other subjects. "In youth," he writes, "her beauty and caprice had occasioned an universal delirium among her young countrymen, and there were still remains of both sufficiently powerful, while she was in England, to render credible their former influence."

That Fanny's detailed despatches delighted her correspondent at Chessington, is only to be expected. "You have produc'd such an illustrious assembly of Princes, and generals, and lords, and ladies, and wits, and pictures, and diamonds, and shoulder-knots, that I feel myself shrink into nothing at the idea of them, — nay, you yourself that made one among them, seem to be a little dazzled at their glare." And then Mr. Crisp rallies her upon her evident admiration of the "beautiful Rauzzini." In another letter there is a

E

significant sentence. "You have learned from that
R[*ogue*] your father (by so long serving as amanuensis,
I suppose) to make your descriptions alive" — an utterance which, while it throws some light on the vexed
question of Miss Burney's style, also recalls us to the
progress of that *History of Music*, in which she bore so
laborious a part. In March 1775 it had come to a
"dead stop" owing to Dr. Burney's rheumatism, which
prevented him from writing; and in April it was
scarcely moving. "My father's History goes on very
slowly indeed at present. . . . He teaches from nine
to nine almost every day, and has scarce time to write
a page a week." Still, it gradually progresses, and in
October, Fanny is able to report that the first volume
is ready. "The History has been this very day, for the
first time since its long cessation, put into the press [?].
It is now *rough* written to the end of the first volume,
Preface and Dedication inclusive. When it is actually
published, we intend to keep the Carnival." A few days
before, the Dedication to the Queen had been read by
Dr. Burney to an admiring friend; and in 1776 the
first volume was issued, when, we may conclude, the
Carnival was duly kept.

But of this, unhappily, no record has been preserved;
and it was some years before a second volume gave
the busy Doctor opportunity for a further jubilation.[1]
Beyond the fact that the Burneys, and Fanny in par-
ticular, made friends (through the Stranges) with the
Miss Paynes, daughters of the famous old bookseller in
Castle Street, "next the Upper Mews-Gate," whose
L-shaped shop was so well known to Eighteenth Century

[1] The second volume appeared in 1782, and the third and fourth
volumes, completing the work, in 1789.

bibliomaniacs,[1] — little remains of interest from the records of 1775. For 1776 there is no journal at all, what had been written having been "destroyed in totality," as consisting wholly of family matters or anecdotes; and save for a very graphic picture of the slatternly Duchess of Devonshire in St. James's Park, no very attractive correspondence, although Mr. Crisp refers to a "conversation piece" which Fanny drew of the fine company at the house of Sir James Lake, the great portrait collector, which should have been good to read. "If specimens of this kind had been preserved of the different *Tons* that have succeeded one another for twenty centuries last past," he writes, "how interesting would they have been! infinitely more so, than antique statues, bas-reliefs, and intaglios." In a fragment dated 2 December there is a vignette of Nollekens the sculptor, "a jolly, fat, lisping, laughing, underbred, good-humoured man as lives: his merit seems pretty much confined to his profession, and his language is as vulgar as his works are elegant." Mrs. Nollekens (the very handsome daughter of Fielding's friend Justice Welch), his wife, is also mentioned: "a civil, obliging, gentle sort of woman; rather too complaisant." Then there is a costume-piece of "Miss B—— *something*, a sister-in-law of Mr. Hayes of the Pantheon," and not entirely unsuggestive of Lady Louisa Larpent in *Evelina;* "a young lady quite *à-la-mode*, — every part of her dress, the very pink and extreme of the fashion; — her [head] erect and stiff as any statue; — her voice low, and delicate, and mincing; — her hair higher than twelve wigs stuck one on the

---

[1] In September, 1785, Miss Sally Payne married Captain James Burney, Fanny's brother.

other; — her waist taper, and pinched evidently; — her eyes cast languishingly from one object to another, and her conversation very much *the thing.*" Decidedly "Daddy" Crisp was right in saying: "To do you justice, Fanny, you paint well!"

For the next year, 1777, there is only one letter to Mr. Crisp; but it is an important one, since it gives Miss Burney's account of her first meeting with Dr. Johnson, to which accident, indeed, it owes its preservation. Dr. Burney had for some time known Johnson slightly, — he had written to him from Lynn with regard to the Dictionary; he had also met him at intervals; and, as we have seen, Johnson, notwithstanding his insensibility to music, had read and appreciated the Musical Tours. Writing Dr. Burney's *Memoirs* in extreme old age, his daughter seems to have thought that Johnson had already accompanied her father to Winchester to put his youngest son, Richard, under the care of the then Head Master of that day, Joseph Warton; and that he had also, before this date, interested himself to procure Dr. Burney access to the libraries at Oxford. But her memory must have led her astray, for both these things, as is plain from Boswell, belong to 1778, while Miss Burney's "first sight" of the great man demonstrably took place on the 20th March, 1777,[1] and came about in this wise. Dr. Burney had been invited by Mr. and Mrs. Thrale to give lessons in music to their eldest daughter, Queenie, afterwards Viscountess Keith. Report says that the lessons were not a great success, since Mrs. Thrale was in the habit of interrupting them sadly in

[1] *Early Diary*, 1889, ii. 153; Birkbeck Hill's *Johnson's Letters*, 1892, ii. 5, and note.

order to talk politics and literature with the clever
Historian of Music. But, as usual, Dr. Burney
speedily became a favourite with all the household;
and, as Johnson was then staying at Streatham, one
of the results was a joint visit by the Doctor and Mrs.
Thrale to St. Martin's Street, which visit was promptly
reported by Fanny for consumption at Chessington.
It took place fourteen years before Boswell's book, and
as printed in the *Early Diary* of 1889, exhibits a fresher
version than that put forward later by the writer herself in the *Memoirs* of her father. No excuse therefore
is needed for giving it the preference here.

"Mrs. and Miss Thrale, Miss Owen, and Mr. Seward
came long before *Lexiphanes*. [This was a name given
to Johnson in 1767, in a little book written to burlesque his style by a Scotch purser named Campbell.]
Mrs. Thrale is a very pretty woman still; she is
extremely lively and chatty; has no supercilious or
pedantic airs, and is really gay and agreeable. Her
daughter [Queenie] is about twelve years old, stiff and
proud, I believe, or else shy and reserved: I don't yet
know which." . . . "My sister Burney [Esther] was
invited to meet and play to them. The conversation
was supported with a good deal of vivacity (N.B. my
father being at home) for about half an hour, and then
Hetty and *Susette*, for the first time *in public*, played a
duet; and in the midst of this performance Dr. Johnson
was announced. He is, indeed, very ill-favoured; is
tall and stout; but stoops terribly; he is almost bent
double. His mouth is almost constantly opening and
shutting, as if he was chewing. He has a strange
method of frequently twirling his fingers, and twisting
his hands. His body is in continual agitation, *see-*

sawing up and down; his feet are never a moment quiet; and, in short, his whole person is in *perpetual motion.* His dress, too, considering the times, and that he had meant to put on his *best becomes,* being engaged to dine in a large company [at Mrs. Montagu's], was as much out of the common road as his figure; he had a large wig, snuff-colour coat, and gold buttons, but no ruffles to his shirt, doughty fists,[1] and black worsted stockings. He is shockingly near-sighted, and did not, till she held out her hand to him, even know Mrs. Thrale. He *poked his nose* over the keys of the harpsichord, till the duet was finished, and then my father introduced Hetty to him as an old acquaintance, and he cordially kissed her! When she was a little girl he had made her a present of *The Idler.*

" His attention, however, was not to be diverted five minutes from the books, as we were in the library; he pored over them, shelf by shelf, almost touching the backs of them with his eye-lashes, as he read their titles. At last, having fixed upon one, he began, without further ceremony, to read to himself, all the time standing at a distance from the company. We were all very much provoked, as we perfectly languished to hear him talk; but it seems he is the most silent creature, when not particularly drawn out, in the world.

" My sister then played another duet with my father; but Dr. Johnson was so deep in the *Encyclopédie* that, as he is very deaf, I question if he even knew what

---

[1] The editor of the *Early Diary* "strongly suspects" that these words in the altered MS. were originally " dirty fists." There are other indications that later corrections have somewhat modified the portrait.

was going forward.   When this was over, Mrs. Thrale, in a laughing manner, said, 'Pray, Dr. Burney, can you tell me what that song was and whose, which Savoi sung last night at Bach's concert, and which you did not hear?'   My father confessed himself by no means so good a diviner, not having had time to consult the stars, though in the house of Sir Isaac Newton. However, wishing to draw Dr. Johnson into some conversation, he told him the question.   The Doctor, seeing his drift, good-naturedly put away his book, and said very drolly, 'And pray, Sir, *who is Bach?* is he a piper?'   Many exclamations of surprise you will believe followed this question.   'Why, you have read his name often in the papers,' said Mrs. Thrale; and then she gave him some account of his Concert, and the number of fine performances she had heard at it.[1]

"'Pray,' said he, gravely, 'Madam, what is the expense?'

"'Oh,' answered she, 'much trouble and solicitation to get a Subscriber's Ticket;— or else half a Guinea.'

"'Trouble and solicitation,' said he, 'I will have nothing to do with; but I would be willing to give eighteen pence.'

"Ha! ha!

"Chocolate being then brought, we adjourned to the drawing-room.   And here, Dr. Johnson being taken from the books, entered freely and most cleverly into conversation; though it is remarkable he never

[1] The Bach referred to was Bach's son, John Christian Bach, or (as he was called) "English" Bach.   He was a famous harpsichord player, who, with Abel of the *viol de gamba*, conducted Mrs. Cornelys' concerts in Soho Square.

speaks at all, but when spoken to; nor does he ever *start*, though he so admirably *supports*, any subject.

"The whole party were engaged to dine at Mrs. Montague's. Dr. Johnson said he had received the most flattering note he had ever read, or that anybody had ever read, by way of invitation. 'Well! so have I too,' cried Mrs. Thrale; 'so if a note from Mrs. Montague is to be boasted of, I beg mine may not be forgot.'

" '*Your* note,' cried Dr. Johnson, 'can bear no comparison with *mine;* I am *at the head of the Philosophers,* she says.'

" 'And I,' cried Mrs. Thrale, '*have all the Muses in my train!*'

" 'A fair battle,' said my father. 'Come, compliment for compliment, and see who will hold out longest!'

" 'Oh, I am afraid for Mrs. Thrale,' cried Mr. Seward, 'for I know Mrs. Montague exerts all her forces, when she attacks Dr. Johnson.'

" 'Oh yes,' said Mrs. Thrale, 'she has often, I know, flattered *him,* till he has been ready to faint.'

" 'Well, ladies,' said my father, 'you must get him between you to-day, and see which can lay on the paint thickest, Mrs. Thrale or Mrs. Montague.'

" 'I had rather,' cried the Doctor, drily, 'go to Bach's Concert.' "

The talk then shifted to Garrick, who, having retired from the stage in the previous year, had been recently reading his farce of *Lethe* to the King and Queen. Dr. Johnson spoke of his old friend and pupil with his wonted candour, and not without touches of critical humour which must have been highly relished by that

still-sore author of *Virginia* to whom Miss Burney's
budget was addressed. Of Garrick's popular faults
Johnson said — " Garrick is accused of vanity; but
few men would have borne such unremitting prosperity
with greater, if with equal moderation.   He is accused,
too, of avarice; but, were he not, he would be accused
of just the contrary; for he now lives rather as *a prince*
than an actor; but the frugality he practised, when he
first appeared in the world, and which, even then, was
perhaps beyond his necessity, has marked his character
ever since; and now, though his table, his equipage
and manner of living, are all the most expensive, and
equal to those of a nobleman, yet the original stain
still blots his name!   Though, had he not fixed upon
himself the charge of avarice, he would long since have
been reproached with luxury and with living beyond
his station in magnificence and splendour."   Another
of the Doctor's animadversions serves to explain an
aspect of the actor's character which has already been
illustrated in this chapter.[1]   " Garrick never enters a
room," he said, " but he regards himself as the object
of general attention, from whom the entertainment
of the company is expected; and true it is, that he
seldom disappoints them; for he has infinite humour,
a very just proportion of wit, and more convivial
pleasantry, than almost any other man.   But then *off*
as well as *on* the Stage, he is always an Actor; for he
thinks it so incumbent on him to be sportive, that his
gaiety becomes mechanical from being habitual, and
he can exert his spirits at all times alike, without con-
sulting his real disposition to hilarity."[2]

Previous to Dr. Johnson's visit to St. Martin's

[1] See *ante*, pp. 38–40.   [2] *Early Diary*, 1889, ii. pp. 153–60.

Street, Miss Burney had been staying at Chessington, whence, to the disgust of Mr. Crisp, she had been hastily recalled to meet her uncle, Mr. Richard Burney of Worcester, whose son Charles her sister Hetty had married. She then went on a visit to her uncle at Barborne (familiarly " Barebones ") Lodge, a little out of Worcester; and here she took part in some private theatricals, playing Mrs. Lovemore in what was apparently the first three-act form of Murphy's *Way to Keep Him*, a comedy in which there are manifest traces of that pioneer sentimental drama, La Chaussée's *Préjugé à-la-mode*—the prejudice in question being, that it is a mistake to love one's wife. She seems, by her own account, to have been terribly nervous (in green and gray); but to have acquitted herself creditably in the crucial third Act. She afterwards appeared as *Huncamunca* in Fielding's burlesque of *Tom Thumb*, the rival character of Glumdalca being taken by her cousin James, and that of Lord Grizzle by Edward Burney the artist. The Tom Thumb of the piece was the youngest of the family, Ann or Nancy, a child of seven, the daughter of Charles Burney and Hetty. By this time Miss Burney had entirely got over her stage fright, and entered thoroughly into her part of Tom Thumb's *fiancée*.

One of the things Huncamunca has to do in *Tom Thumb* is to express her anxiety to be married. It is not, however, this unbecoming aspiration (upon which Miss Burney was of course afterwards sufficiently rallied) that prompts the "Oh! Huncamunca, Huncamunca, oh!" of Fielding's parody of Thomson. But the point serves to remind us that, in this chapter, nothing has been said of Miss Burney's admirers.

Scattered through her Journal are various fugitive references to different gentlemen, old and young, who were evidently attracted by her vivacity and charm, shy and demure as she professed to be. But she had not yet realised her own ambition and fallen seriously in love. "I am too much spoilt," she says, "by such men as my father and Mr. Crisp to content myself with a character merely inoffensive." These words were written of an importunate suitor, with the unpromising name of Thomas Barlow, who made his appearance early in May, 1775. He seems to have been very much in earnest, indeed, — to use the expression of Mr. Toots, of whom he somehow contrives to remind us, — to have been "perfectly sore" with devotion. His ardent, or (as he terms it) "ardurous" Pen addresses to Miss Burney several long-winded and very alembicate epistles, but she will have none of him, although, strange to say, nearly all her family, including the paternal Crisp, — who was particularly urgent that she should not lose a chance of establishing herself, — favour Mr. Barlow's pretensions. But, as she very sensibly tells Mr. Crisp, she is "determined never to marry without having the very highest value and esteem for the man who should be her lord." And Mr. Barlow, besides that he is "extremely precipitate," does not "hit her fancy." So there is no more to say.

Upon the whole, when it is remembered that this retiring but observant young lady of five-and-twenty had a travelled sailor brother, and two sisters who had been educated at Paris; — that she had seen the town and country both in London and King's Lynn; — that she had read Richardson and Marivaux and Sterne,

if not Fielding; — that she knew Sir Joshua and
Nollekens, and was familiar with the acting of Garrick,
both on and off the stage ; — that she had heard Agujari
at her best, and the Gabrielli at her worst; — that she
had been introduced to Dr. Johnson and Mrs. Thrale;
— that she had conversed with Otaheitan Omai, eaten
roast apples with Abyssinian Bruce, and been allowed
to inspect what Horace Walpole calls the "infamous
diamonds" of the veneered barbarian, Alexis Orloff, —
it will, we think, be admitted that her experience of
things in general had been of a very varied kind.
If to this be added that she was a copious and diligent
diarist; — the sworn "anecdote-monger" of a distant
correspondent ; — and the faithful secretary of a scribbling father — it must also be granted that she was by
no means ill-equipped for the production of that work
of fiction to the story of which the ensuing chapter is
devoted.

CHAPTER III

At the beginning of 1778, English Literature, and
especially that branch of it which consists of fiction,
seems to have been suffering from a kind of sleeping
sickness. The great masters who had followed upon
Richardson's success with *Pamela*, were gone, — as was
Richardson himself. Fielding, whose last novel of
Amelia had appeared in 1751, was dead, and his far
younger rival, Smollett, whose *Humphry Clinker* came
twenty years later, was also dead. Sterne was dead;
Goldsmith was dead; and both *Tristram Shandy* and
the *Vicar of Wakefield* had been a considerable time
before the public. Johnson, whose *Rasselas* dated
from 1759, and Horace Walpole, whose *Castle of Otranto*
dated from 1764, were the only living writers of fiction
of any eminence, for it is impossible to give a very
high place to the *Julia de Roubigné* of Sterne's tearful
imitator, Henry Mackenzie, or to the *Champion of
Virtue*, which Walpole's disciple, Miss Clara Reeve,
afterwards re-named *The Old English Baron*. Both
of these, however, belong to 1777. Apart from them,
there is nothing that rises above the average level
of the

> "books in marble covers
> About smart girls and dapper lovers,"

61

which formed the staple product of the Circulating
Library, — those "*Ventures* of Jack this, and the
History of Betsy t'other, and Sir Humphrys, and
women with hard Christian names," which exercised
the Nurse in Colman's *Polly Honeycombe.* "And then"
— says the Author in his Prologue —

> "And then so *sentimental* is the Stile,
> So chaste, yet so bewitching all the while!
> Plot, and elopement, passion, rape, and rapture,
> The total sum of ev'ry dear — dear — Chapter."

Of these latter and minor performances, perhaps the
only one which — for the moment — deserves a passing mention is the *Excursion* of Mrs. Frances Brooke,
already referred to in Chapter I. as the popular author
of *Lady Julia Mandeville.* The *Excursion* has a certain
faint interest from the fact that, preceding *Evelina*
only by a few months, it deals, to some extent, with
a similar theme, since the heroine is described as " a
young lady of family but small fortune, with a mind
sensible and improved, but totally ignorant of the
world," who " launches out from the country, steer-
ing without a pilot or compass, through the rocks
and shelves of a London life." One of her perils is,
of course, a heartless young nobleman, educated by
his father "upon the detestable plan " of my Lord
Chesterfield, whose *Miscellaneous Works* had then just
been issued by Dr. Maty. Fanny Burney knew Mrs.
Brooke's books, and had indeed made her personal
acquaintance, both in the studio of Miss Catherine
Reid, the " English Rosalba," and at the Opera House
in the Haymarket, of which Mrs. Brooke was co-lessee
with the actress, Mary Ann Yates. "Mrs. Brooke
is very short and fat, and squints "— writes Fanny of

their first interview, " but has the art of showing agreeable ugliness. She is very well bred, and expresses
herself with much modesty upon all subjects ; which
in an *authoress*, a woman of *known* understanding, is
extremely pleasing." But save and except the very
superficial resemblance referred to above, there is no
trace of any connection between the *Excursion* and
Evelina. Indeed, as for the *Excursion*, although
Sylvanus Urban contrives to give it a review of two
or three columns, — a far longer notice than he afterwards, and very tardily, accorded to *Evelina*, — it is
not more readable to-day than the same author's *Lady
Julia Mandeville*, or her translations from the French,
— that is to say, it is not readable at all.

It has already been stated in Chapter I. that, amid
the fuel of Miss Burney's Poland Street holocaust, was
" an entire work of fiction." This was *The History of
Caroline Evelyn*, of which we know no more than is told
us in the Preface to *The Wanderer* and the *Memoirs of
Dr. Burney.* It was " the last of the little works that
was immolated," and contained the history of Evelina's
mother, who, as appears from the later novel dealing
with her daughter's entrance into the world, was the
only child of a gentleman of birth and education
named Evelyn. Mr. Evelyn having been unwise
enough to marry a good-looking waitress at a tavern,
had in consequence migrated to France, where he
died. His daughter Caroline, after being brought up
carefully by his old tutor, the Rev. Mr. Villars, was
sent for to Paris by her vulgar mother, who by this
time had married again, her second husband being a
Frenchman named Duval. Oppressed by Mme. Duval,
and menaced with an unsuitable partner, Miss Evelyn

rashly consented to marry, without witnesses, a profligate young baronet, Sir John Belmont, who brought her back to England. Here, after the approved fashion of profligate young baronets in novels, he, in due time, destroyed the marriage certificate, denying that the ceremony had ever taken place. His broken-hearted wife sought an asylum with her old guardian, Mr. Villars, and subsequently died in giving birth to Evelina.

Such is the *History of Caroline Evelyn*, as it is summarised in the opening letters of her daughter's story; and such, we may imagine, in expanded form, must have been the matter of the manuscript which was burnt. Whatever was the precise date of its destruction, it must obviously have been a very juvenile performance. It was certainly written before its author had begun her Journal — in other words, before she had begun, not only to record her thoughts and feelings, but to take intelligent stock of the variations of humanity; and it must also have been written before she had been subjected to the discipline of acting as private secretary to her father. As to the plot, there was nothing in that beyond the ability of an imaginative schoolgirl. Unfortunate heroine, heartless parent, profligate baronet, private marriage, burnt certificate, — these were the conventional material of contemporary fiction, if indeed they did not come direct from *Grandison* or *Clarissa*. What would be interesting to know is, whether the *History of Caroline Evelyn* contained any promise of character-drawing, still more of social satire and humorous incident. We suspect it did not. In all likelihood, it was merely a sentimental exercise in the taste which then represented the degradation of the Richardsonian method, as modified by French imitators; and perhaps aimed at nothing more than mild rivalry of the existing biographies of *Miss Polly Willis*, *Miss Lucy Wellers*, *Miss Charlotte Villars*, and the rest of the ingenious works enumerated at the end of the Preface to *Polly Honeycombe*.

There is no doubt that when Fanny Burney made dutiful sacrifice of the *History of Caroline Evelyn*, she sincerely intended, in her own words, "to extinguish for ever in its ashes her scribbling propensity." But *qui a bu, boira.* As we have seen, the checked impulse almost immediately found its outlet in keeping a journal; and to keep a journal was but, in another form, to exercise the prohibited gift and to gratify the old ambition. The fire which "consumed her productions, extirpated neither the invention nor the inclination that had given them birth"; and, as time went on, she felt herself more and more disposed to revert to her first conception, and to brood over the singular situation in which Miss Evelyn's daughter must find herself "between the elegant connections of her mother, and the vulgar ones of her grandmother." Irresistibly and almost insensibly, she felt the whole story forming itself gradually in her mind, and calling urgently to be written down, long before a syllable was committed to paper. When she actually began to write, is not clear. It was in 1768 that the diary opened; but there are no hints of the composition of *Evelina* for some time to come. Probably it was written by fits and starts; and grew but very gradually into shape, making its greatest progress during its writer's visits to Chessington, or in the leisure procured during her father's two absences on

F

the continent. And much of it was no doubt penned
in Newton's old observatory, remote from her step-
mother's watchful eye.

It must have been in 1776, after the publication of
the first volume of Dr. Burney's *History of Music*, that
Fanny began definitely to think of print. Having
been long accustomed to act as secretary for her
father, she grew apprehensive lest her ordinary script
should be recognised at press; and she therefore proceeded to transcribe her work "in a feigned hand."
"The fear of discovery," she writes, "or of suspicion
in the house, made the copying extremely laborious
to me; for in the daytime, I could only take odd
moments, so that I was obliged to sit up the greatest
part of many nights, in order to get it ready." By
the time two volumes were completed, she was
sufficiently tired out — with "all this *fagging*" — to
wish to know whether her labour was likely to be in
vain. She accordingly wrote a letter to Dodsley of
Pall Mall, without signature, offering him what she
had already prepared, and promising to transmit the
remainder in the following year. The reply was to
be addressed to the Orange Coffee House in the Haymarket, under cover to an imaginary "Mr. Grafton."
Dodsley's answer was to the effect that he could not
consider the work without being informed of the
author's name. Thereupon Fanny, and her only con-
fidantes, her sisters, after sitting in committee upon
this discouraging reply, decided that it would be
wiser to try a less fashionable publisher. They fixed
upon Mr. Thomas Lowndes of 77 Fleet Street, who
expressed a desire to see the manuscript. It was
accordingly carried to Fleet Street, "in the dark of

the evening," by Fanny's brother Charles, who, having been admitted to the secret, was disguised for the occasion by his sisters in appropriate costume. But the bookseller's reply, though one which might have been expected, was a disappointment. Mr. Lowndes informed his correspondent at the Orange Coffee House, that, while (with some reservations) he approved the instalment submitted, he could not think of printing the book until it was finished; and that he would consequently await the author's pleasure, hoping to receive it as soon as it was ready for type.

Here was a blow which, for the moment, suspended all further progress. "I had hardly time," says Fanny, "to write half a page in a day; and neither my health nor inclination would allow me to continue my *nocturnal* scribbling for so long a time, as to write first, and then copy, a whole volume."[1] Nevertheless, she must have gone on with it at intervals. In March, 1777, when, as already related, she went to Chessington, she was certainly at work upon it. "Distant as you may think us from the great world," she writes to her sister Susan, "I sometimes find myself in the midst of it, though nobody suspects the brilliancy of the company I occasionally keep." This is a transparent reference to the characters of the book upon which she was engaged. In April, she went to Worcester; and before starting, appears to have determined that the time had arrived when she must divulge her secret to her father. Hitherto she had never taken any serious step without his knowledge; and on this occasion had refrained from obtaining his

---

[1] This suggests that, at the beginning of 1777, the *third* volume was not yet composed.

concurrence, first from an unwillingness to acknow-
ledge her authorship, and secondly, from a dread that
he might ask to see what she had written. Upon this
latter head, however, she was speedily reassured.
Although Dr. Burney — who, we must remember, was
wholly without previous information on the subject
— treated the communication very lightly, he was
evidently surprised. In amused compliance with his
daughter's urgent appeal for secrecy, he nevertheless
forbore even to ask the title of the book, or to make
any further enquiries. He only requested to be informed, from time to time, of its progress towards
completion; and then left Fanny to follow her own
devices. Probably he thought no more of the matter.
Preoccupied with his own affairs, he can have attached
but slight importance to the intelligence conveyed to
him; and certainly never dreamed that his daughter's
attempt would be attended with success. And so
Fanny, having liberated her mind, and eased her filial
conscience, set off for Worcester.

When she got back to St. Martin's Street, she
finished the preparation of vol. iii., which was handed
to Mr. Lowndes, who, in a few days, offered £20 for
the manuscript, — " an offer which was accepted with
alacrity, and boundless surprise at its magnificence,"
by the anonymous author.[1] The next we hear of the
book is in the middle of January, 1778. About this
date, Edward Burney, the artist, who had been pro-
moted to the post of confidential agent in place of his
cousin Charles, then in the country, arrived with news

[1] After the third edition (1779) Lowndes paid her another £10,
making £30 in all (*Memoirs of Dr. Burney*, 1832, ii. 151).

that a parcel was waiting for " Mr. Grafton " at the
Orange Coffee House. It proved to contain a printed
but incomplete and unbound copy of *Evelina,* which
was accompanied by a letter from Mr. Lowndes,
requesting that a " List of Errata " might be supplied
without delay. This was accordingly done; and the
book was returned to the publisher, by whom, shortly
afterwards, it was advertised in the *London Chronicle*
for January 27–9, and elsewhere, as on sale, in three
volumes, 12mo, price 7s. 6d. sewed, and 9s. bound,
under the title of *Evelina; or, A Young Lady's Entrance
into the World.* Mrs. Burney read out the announce-
ment at the St. Martin's Street breakfast table; but,
being ignorant of the circumstances, naturally failed to
detect the signs of intelligence which passed between
Fanny and her sisters. Whether Dr. Burney was
present, is not recorded; but as he did not know the
name of the book, what was to its writer the earliest
notification of its public appearance would probably
have escaped his attention. For some weeks nothing
more was heard of the matter, although, in March, the
sisters and their cousin Edward, making enquiry at
Bell's Library in the Strand, found that *Evelina* was in
circulation; and that, as Fanny puts it, " a work which
was so lately lodged in all privacy in her bureau, was
now to be seen by every butcher and baker, cobbler and
tinker, throughout the three kingdoms for the small
tribute of three pence." After this, Dr. Burney fell
ill of fever. Having helped to nurse him, Fanny herself had inflammation of the lungs; and, in May, went
off to Chessington to recruit. It was at Chessington
that she received, at this late hour, the first copy of
her book, for which she had hitherto applied unsuc-

cessfully to Mr. Lowndes. He now forwarded a set
"most elegantly bound" (which may be taken as an
indication that it was growing in popularity), and this
copy was apparently followed by ten further copies.
Some time, however, was still to elapse before *Evelina*
became thoroughly well known, and we may occupy
the interval with an examination of its contents.[1]

The plot is neither very original nor very intricate.
With the parentage and early history of the heroine,
Evelina Anville or, more properly, Belmont, the reader
has already been made acquainted. At the beginning
of the story, her low-born grandmother, Mme. Duval,
having ignored her for seventeen years, has begun to
show disquieting signs of seeking to obtain control
over her, much to the dismay of her guardian, the
excellent Mr. Villars. But nothing happens until
Mr. Villars, having permitted Evelina to visit his
and her friend, Lady Howard, at Howard Grove, is
unwillingly persuaded to let her accompany Lady
Howard's daughter, Mrs. Mirvan, on a visit to London.
Mrs. Mirvan is going to town to meet her husband, a
Captain in the Navy, newly returned from a seven-years'
absence on a distant station. They take lodgings in
Queen-Anne-Street, Cavendish Square. From this point
Evelina mainly holds the pen. Almost as a matter of
course, one of the first persons they encounter is Mme.
Duval, travelling with a Frenchman named Du Bois.
(Du Bois, it may be mentioned in parenthesis, was
the name of Fanny's Huguenot grandfather.) To
Mrs. Mirvan's aristocratic acquaintances, Mme. Duval
speedily opposes her own vulgar connections, the

---

[1] *Diary and Letters*, 1892, i. 10; *Memoirs of Dr. Burney*,
1832, ii. 149; *Early Diary*, 1889, ii. 239 n.

Branghtons, a silversmith's family on Snow-Hill, with whom, in due time, originates the suggestion that "Miss," as they call Evelina, shall endeavour to obtain recognition by her father, — an idea which obviously has its source in their desire to secure Mme. Duval's fortune for themselves. At the instance of Mme. Duval, then staying at Howard Grove, Lady Howard writes to Sir John Belmont, who returns an answer from the studious ambiguity of which it is impossible to extract anything but a rather contemptuous negative. The Mirvans, who have been temporising with Mme. Duval in order to keep Evelina with them as long as possible, are now obliged to surrender her for a time to her objectionable grandmother, by whom she is carried to London and her Snow-Hill cousins. Eventually she returns to Mr. Villars. But during her stay in Holborn, she has become acquainted with one of the Branghtons' lodgers, a young Scotchman in destitute circumstances, named Macartney, whom she saves from suicide. In Paris Macartney has fallen in love with a beautiful English girl, the alleged daughter of a baronet, who turns out to be Sir John Belmont himself. This girl is a certain Bessie Green, who has been palmed off upon his paternal remorse as Caroline Evelyn's child. Finally, at Bath, things come right. While Evelina is there on a visit, her father arrives to drink the waters, accompanied by the pseudo-Miss Belmont. But Evelina's striking resemblance to her dead mother is unmistakable; she is at once acknowledged by Sir John Belmont with appropriate heroics, and at the close of volume three, bestows her hand upon Lord Orville, the best of a fair number of eligible and ineligible suitors.

This, reduced to an outline, is the plot of Miss
Burney's story ; and that it has any special novelty of
construction, can scarcely be contended.   Nor, although
she has adopted the " epistolary Style " of Richardson,
can it be said to bear any great likeness to the work
of that master.   There is no endeavour after mental
analysis ; or — it may be added — any obtrusive evidence of prolixity.   The book does not, like the
novels of Fielding and Smollett, deal with humanity
in the rough ; but rather with humanity in the cir-
cumscribed arena of domestic life.   Its distinctive
merit consists in the skill and graphic power of the
character drawing ; in the clever contrast of the
different individuality ; in the author's keen if somewhat crude sense of the ridiculous ; and, above all, in
the sprightliness and vivacity of her narrative, especially when she writes in the person of the heroine.
And this last, in great measure, is due to the fact that
in Evelina Miss Burney has portrayed her younger self.
Until the publication of the *Early Diary*, this, though
conjectured, was not clearly established.   But a perusal
of the letters to Mr. Crisp, of the Teignmouth and
Worcester Journals, and of half a dozen of the reported
conversations, shows clearly that Evelina Anville,
narrating her adventures to Mr. Villars, was using
very much the same pen as Frances Burney had employed for those *nouvelles à-la-main* which, from time
to time, she despatched to " Daddy " Crisp at Chessington.   The writer who describes the theatricals at
Barborne Lodge, or recounts the long conversations
with Mr. Barlow, is precisely the same person who, in
the novel, reproduces the small talk in the tea-room
at the Pantheon, or records the rough-and-tumble

misadventures of Mme. Duval at Ranelagh. All these
people and places Miss Burney had seen; or if she had
not, it needed little but her perceptive faculty, her
sense of humour, and her dramatising gift, to enable
her to invent similar characters, and exhibit them in
action.

It is possible, of course, that, in some cases, Miss
Burney leaned upon her predecessors, especially where
her own experiences fell short. Lord Orville, it has
been suggested, is a recollection of the hero of *Sir
Charles Grandison;* Sir Clement Willoughby, of Sir
Hargrave Pollexfen or Mr. Greville in the same novel.
That she should think of these then-established types
would, indeed, be only natural. But while Richardson
drew his male heroes mainly from his moral conscious-
ness, Miss Burney has rectified her puppets from her
personal recollections. Lord Orvilles, perhaps, were
not very common in her environment. Still, to say
nothing of King in Lord Ogleby (she knew the
Clandestine Marriage by heart), she had seen and heard
a live fine gentleman in Fulke Greville; and in Mr.
Anthony Chamier and Mr. Charles Boone had conversed with some flesh-and-blood specimens of men
of the world, who helped to make her characters,
objectively at all events, more convincingly real than
those of Richardson. For Lord Orville — though
somewhat shadowy — is really a nobleman; and Sir
Clement Willoughby, a not-inconceivable specimen of
the *genus* "agreeable rake." As to the impertinent
fop, Mr. Lovel, one can imagine that she would have
little difficulty in constructing him — with an added
sprinkle of malice — out of the "scraps and heel-taps"
of her coxcomb cousin, Richard Burney of Worcester,

or of that other fantastic feather-head, the Spanish
traveller, Mr. Twiss. But the Lovels, and the Orvilles,
and the Willoughbys, clever as they are, would scarcely
have made the fortune of *Evelina;* still less would
the benedictory Mr. Villars, the exemplary Lady
Howard, Mrs. Mirvan and her daughter, or that
melancholy concession to sentimentalism, Mr. Macartney. These belong to the working machinery of
the story; its prominent interest, apart from its
accurate pictures of contemporary character and
manners, is concentrated upon the two antagonists,
Captain Mirvan and Mme. Duval, and upon the
inimitably vulgar Branghton group, which includes
the Holborn beau, Mr. Smith.

Madame Duval, in particular, is drawn with remarkable vigour, though it is difficult to imagine
how, at any period of her life, an educated man could
possibly have married her. Her illiterate English
with its cheap French tags, her *Ma fois* and her
Shakespearean superlatives, all combine to make a
most graphic broad-comedy portrait. She would perhaps have been better for a touch, which Goldsmith
would certainly not have omitted, of tenderness some-
where; as it is, the only sign of anything approaching
that quality is her solicitude for M. Du Bois, the poor
French gentleman who accompanies her, — one hardly
knows why, — for he has no very definite purpose in
the book beyond swelling the list of Evelina's admirers,
and opposing his courtesy and unobtrusive good manners to the rudeness of his immediate associates. But
though no softer traits make us admire Mme. Duval,
one can at least be sorry for her. A certain amount
of horse-play — and even the ruining of a new Lyons

silk costume — are perhaps permissible in a roaring
farce; but to drag an elderly woman forcibly along
the high road, shake her furiously, deposit her in a
ditch (bumping her vigorously the while), and then
tie her feet together, leaving her "almost roaring, and
in the utmost agony of rage and terror" — certainly
seems to be going to unusual lengths in the pur-
suit of practical joking, even with a person who has
so far forgotten herself as to spit in your face. If
Mme. Duval was not a person of "position" in one
sense, she was at least (as the Colonel says in *Punch*)
a person of exceedingly "uncomfortable position"
in another. Yet, as Miss Burney has depicted the
episode, we must presume that she has actually
depicted something she had heard of or seen. And
there is no doubt that there was an under side to the
often superficial and conventional refinement of her
day, — a side of absolute heartlessness and insensibility,
begotten of brutal pastimes, butcherly penal laws, and
a cynical disregard for the value of human life. Even
in that admirable comedy of Goldsmith which Miss
Burney had seen played not so very many years before
the appearance of *Evelina*, there are traces of this,
though Goldsmith was the most amiable of men. Yet
even Goldsmith allows Tony Lumpkin to tell an audience that, after jolting two ladies, one of them his
own mother, to a jelly, he has finally lodged them in
a horsepond; and everyone seems to think the joke
an excellent one. Nor are there any indications that
Johnson or Reynolds ever commented upon the callous
barbarity of the proceeding.

This being so, we could perhaps hardly expect any
superfine delicacy from the rough sailor whom Miss

Burney has invented for Mme. Duval's discomfiture. Captain Mirvan is an officer of the Oakum and Hatchway type rather than of the Lieutenant Bowling order. His twin aversions are a fop and a Frenchman; and he meets them both; or rather, in place of the latter, he meets an Englishwoman naturalised in France, which does as well. Indeed, it is a little curious that, in his hatred of "Madam Frog," as he calls Evelina's grandmother, Captain Mirvan entirely overlooks the fact that Mme. Duval is really nothing more than a vulgar English barmaid. Captain Mirvan is excellently conceived, but only partially exhibited. To say nothing of the fact that he is a seaman on shore, it would have been impossible for Evelina to depict him except in expurgated form. She herself allows as much to Mr. Villars. "Notwithstanding the attempts I so frequently make of writing some of the Captain's conversation, I can only give you a faint idea of his language; for almost every other word he utters, is accompanied by an oath, which, I am sure, would be as unpleasant for you to read, as for me to write. And, besides, he makes use of a thousand sea-terms, which are to me quite unintelligible." Miss Burney had a brother who was a lieutenant in the navy, and no doubt was sufficiently instructed as to the manners and customs of the mariners of Cook's day. She moreover appreciated to the full their delight in hoaxes and practical jokes. As regards their oaths and asseverations no one can blame her reticence, — a reticence which was commended even by her contemporaries. But it is permissible to criticism to observe that a Georgian ship-captain *ad usum Delphini* and deprived in great

measure of his picturesque nautical jargon is an
artistic contradiction which it is difficult to invest
with complete and convincing reality. It is no
doubt owing in part to the absence of his uncouth
amphibious atmosphere that Captain Mirvan's baiting
of Mme. Duval leaves such an unpleasantly cold-
blooded impression upon the modern reader. On
ship-board, and in his own element, he was no doubt
a brave man and a smart officer. On shore, he is an
unmitigated bear; and since Mme. Duval was in a
way his guest, an absolutely inconceivable host.

Of the Branghton family, Miss Burney has given,
at the outset, a rather fuller introductory description
than she usually gives of her characters. The father,
Mme. Duval's nephew, is a silversmith on Snow Hill,
a man about forty, intelligent, but contracted and
prejudiced, having spent his life in the city, and contemptuous of all who reside elsewhere. His son is
"weaker in his understanding, and more gay in his
temper; but his gaiety is that of a foolish, over-grown
schoolboy, whose mirth consists in noise and disturbance. He disdains his father for his close attention
to business, and love of money; though he seems himself to have no talents, spirit, or generosity, to make
him superior to either. His chief delight appears
to be tormenting and ridiculing his sisters, who, in
return, most heartily despise him." The elder girl
is not ill-looking; but is proud, ill-tempered and con-
ceited. " She hates the city, though without knowing
why; for it is easy to discover she has lived nowhere
else." The younger sister, Polly, is "rather pretty,
very foolish, very ignorant, very giddy and very good
natured." This worshipful family, after the fashion

of the eighteenth century, live at the shop in the city, and let some of the rooms. One of the garrets is occupied by the already mentioned Scotch poet, Macartney, while the dining room is in possession of the Holborn beau, who, besides keeping a foot-boy of his own, is — according to Miss Polly Branghton — "quite like one of the quality, and dresses as fine, and goes to balls and dances, and everything quite in taste." Mr. Smith, with his underbred gentility and his awkward sprightliness, is the most vivid of the portraits in the book.

With enforced associates of this type, it is easy to conceive that Evelina is continually involved in vexation and embarrassment, and even landed in some equivocal situations. The Branghtons take her to the Opera, but carry her to the shilling gallery. They take her to Vauxhall, where, unlike Goldsmith's pawnbroker's widow, she *does* contrive to see the famous waterworks. But by the heedlessness of her cousins, she is decoyed into the dubious Dark Walks, where she is rescued from a gang of rakes by Sir Clement Willoughby, only to be subsequently subjected by him to impertinent gallantries on his own account. After this, she goes to a ball at the Long Room at Hampstead with Mme. Duval, where she has the greatest difficulty in avoiding to " hop a dance " with the importunate Holborn beau, who, in the phrase of his circle, is " as fine as fivepence." At Marylebone Gardens an explosion of M. Torré's fireworks terrifies her into seeking the protection of some very undesirable companions of her own sex, in whose compromising company, to her intense annoyance, she is discovered both by Lord Orville and Sir Clement

Willoughby. Finally, after she has been pestered
by the attentions of Mr. Smith, and threatened by
Mme. Duval with young Branghton as a husband,
the full measure of her mortification is filled at
Kensington Gardens, where, in a soaking shower, her
cousins contrive to borrow Lord Orville's coach, in
her name, although against her will. As a result the
coach is badly injured in taking these discreditable
connections to Snow Hill. There are other consequences to this misadventure, but they cannot be
touched upon here.

These scenes at the old London pleasure resorts of
Evelina's century — as was admitted by her contemporaries — are depicted with full knowledge, and with
a spirit and animation not to be found elsewhere,
though it is difficult to make quotation from them
without presenting them imperfectly. One passage,
however, which Johnson admired, we may venture to
cite, with the *caveat* that a brick is not a building.
The party are in the Great Room at Vauxhall, looking
at one of Hayman's paintings; — we may assume it,
from the reference to Neptune, to be that which com-
memorated Admiral Hawke's defeat of the French in
Quiberon Bay. Evelina has asked M. Du Bois for an
explanation of the subject: Mme. Duval invokes the
assistance of Mr. Smith, who, for the moment, is sorely
crestfallen at the superior ease and splendour of Sir
Clement Willoughby : —

"'Don't ask him [M. Du Bois]' — she cries — 'your
best way is to ask Mr. Smith, for he's been here the
oftenest. Come, Mr. Smith, I daresay you can tell us
all about them.'

"'Why, yes, Ma'am, yes,' said Mr. Smith : who,

brightening up at this application, advanced towards us, with an air of assumed importance, which, however, sat very uneasily upon him, and begged to know what he should explain first: 'For I have attended,' said he, 'to all these paintings, and know everything in them perfectly well; for I am rather fond of pictures, Ma'am; and, really, I must say, I think a pretty picture is a — a very — is really a very — is something very pretty —'

" 'So do I too,' said Madame Duval, 'but pray now, Sir, tell us who that is meant for,' pointing to a figure of Neptune.

" 'That! — Why, that, Ma'am, is, — . . . I can't think how I come to be so stupid, but really I have forgot his name; — and yet, I know it as well as my own too, — however, he's a *General*, Ma'am, they are all Generals.'

"I saw Sir Clement bite his lips; and, indeed, so did I mine.

" 'Well,' said Madame Duval, 'it's the oddest dress for a general ever I see!'

" 'He seems so capital a figure,' said Sir Clement to Mr. Smith, 'that I imagine he must be *Generalissimo* of the whole army.'

" 'Yes, Sir, yes,' answered Mr. Smith, respectfully bowing, and highly delighted at being thus referred to, 'you are perfectly right;—but I cannot for my life think of his name; — perhaps, Sir, you may remember it?'

" 'No, really,' replied Sir Clement, 'my acquaintance among the generals is not so extensive.'

"The ironical tone of voice in which Sir Clement spoke, entirely disconcerted Mr. Smith; who again

retiring to a humble distance, seemed sensibly morti-
fied at the failure of the attempt to recover his
consequence."

After volume two, we hear little of Mme. Duval
or the Branghtons; and Captain Mirvan only appears
at the end of the book for the exposure of the
fop, Mr. Lovel, which he accomplishes with his customary cruelty. Croker thought this latter part
" very tedious," but his objection was not shared by
Miss Burney's first readers. There are, it is true, no
characters in it as broadly drawn as Captain Mirvan
and Mme. Duval; but those that are new, have all
the trick of the time. Lord Merton and Mr. Coverley
are typical examples of the Georgian man of pleasure,
and the race of old women by which they settle their
wager, could easily, painful as it seemed to the lookers-
on, have been paralleled from the annals of the day.
Indeed, something of the kind was devised by Garrick
for the diversions of his Hampton Villa. Lady Louisa
Larpent is an excellent specimen of the die-away,
lackadaisical lady of quality who must have abounded
at the old watering places, while the remorseless Mrs.
Selwyn, secure in her age and independent means, and
devoting herself entirely to the reckless gratification
of her caustic humour, is again a thoroughly recognis-
able society type. In fact, these latter personages
are truer to the social conditions of the day than
even " Madam French " and the Captain, and only
failed of equal applause because they were less novel.
So far from being tedious, the last volume seems to
us the most easily written. The intrigue, slight as
it is, is artfully entangled, and the style has the
additional freedom which might be expected from

G

the fact that there was now a definite publisher in
sight, as soon as the work should be brought to
an end.

Prefixed to *Evelina* is a votive poem of five quatrains,
a "Dedication addressed to the Authors of the *Monthly*
and *Critical Reviews*," and a Preface. The verses,
although headed "To **** *****," are of course
intended for Dr. Burney.

> "Oh ! of my life at once the source and joy !
>   If e'er thy eyes these feeble lines survey,
>   Let not their folly their intent destroy ;
>   Accept the tribute — but forget the lay " —

they conclude, and it would be idle to pretend that
their affection is not more manifest than their poetical
merit. The "Dedication" and the "Preface," on the
contrary, are well invented; and moreover, shew plainly
that, in serious or impersonal prose, the Johnsonian
standard, afterwards so obtrusive in the writer's work,
was already present to her mind. Speaking, in the
Preface, of her predecessors in fiction, she says, "I yet
presume not to attempt pursuing the same ground which
they have tracked; whence, though they may have
cleared the weeds, they have also culled the flowers ;
and, though they have rendered the path plain, they
have left it barren." Again, "Whatever may be the fate
of these letters, the writer is satisfied they will meet
with justice ; and commends them to the press, though
hopeless of fame, yet not regardless of censure." These
are sentences which, with their balanced turn, and contrast of clauses, might have come direct from *Rasselas*
or the *Rambler*. The same Preface contains a passage
to which we are probably indebted for much of that old

persistent misconception as to the author's age, of which
Croker ("no one could lash a woman like Rigby!")
made such paltry capital. " To draw characters from
nature, though not from life, and to mark the manners
of the times, is the attempted plan of the following
letters. For this purpose, a young female, educated
in the most secluded retirement, makes, *at the age of
seventeen* [the italics are ours], her first appearance upon
the great and busy stage of life." Here, no doubt,
is the source and origin of the story which Croker
had "always seen and heard stated." To any unpre-
judiced mind, it must be obvious that Miss Burney
is referring, not to her own age, but to that of her
heroine; and this is confirmed — if confirmation were
needed — by her Diary. " I have not pretended," she
writes in March, 1778, "to shew the world what it
actually *is*, but what it *appears* to a girl of seventeen: —
and so far as that, surely any girl who is *past* seventeen may safely do?" And yet, as late as 1871, a
critic was found to quote the words of the " Preface "
and to contend, in Croker's interest, that Miss Burney
was speaking of herself.[1]

The first of the Reviews to answer the appeal in the
Dedication was not either of those to which the author
had referred. In the *London Review* for February there
was a tiny notice of three lines. But, considering that
it came from, or was approved by, the critic whom
Macaulay stigmatises as the "envious Kenrick," it was
not unfriendly. "There was much more merit" in
Evelina's history, it said, " as well respecting style,
character and incident, than was generally to be found

[1] Forsyth, *Novels and Novelists of the Eighteenth Century*,
1871, p. 325.

among our modern novels." The *Monthly Review* (Mr. Ralph Griffiths) was the next to take up the book, making its report in April. This was not long; but it was excellent. It pronounced *Evelina* to be "one of the most sprightly, entertaining, and agreeable productions" of the kind which had of late fallen under its notice. It praised the "great variety of natural incidents," and declared the characters to be "agreeably diversified, conceived and drawn with propriety, and supported with spirit." "The whole," it went on, "is written with great ease, and command of language. From this commendation, however, we must except the character of a son of Neptune, whose manners are rather those of a rough uneducated country squire, than those of a genuine sea captain." For the *Critical Review* Miss Burney had to wait until September, when Sylvanus Urban also joined the concert. The notice in the *Critical Review* was the longest of all. It compared the writer with Richardson. It considered the first and third volumes to be the best, and it praised Mme. Duval and Captain Mirvan as, in great measure, original. With respect to the author, whom it speaks of as "he," it was still wholly in the dark; and it commended the knowledge of the world and the experience of life which the book contained. Mr. Urban contented himself with a long extract from the "Preface," and concluded, "Such is the just account given of this work by the author; to which we shall only add that these vols. will afford a pleasing innocent amusement, exhibiting, in an easy style, many such characters as occur in the world, not raised so high as to be extravagant, nor sunk so low as to be disgusting."

There is no definite evidence that Miss Burney had

any knowledge either of Kenrick's or Griffiths' review, when, in May, she went to Chessington. While she was at "Daddy" Crisp's — as already related — the first bound copy was received from Lowndes. But those in the secret had kept it well, and it was not until June that it was really revealed. In March, Fanny's cousin Richard, recovering from an illness, had heard *Evelina* read aloud, and was taken into confidence; while in May, his sister Bessy, one of the actors in the Worcester theatricals, had, in her own phrase, "smoked" Fanny in the new book, which was beginning to be talked about. But Fanny's father, to whom *Evelina* was dedicated, was still wholly ignorant of the matter, and his diffident daughters did not dare to undeceive him. At last, at the beginning of June, Charlotte writes jubilantly that Papa has been looking at the review in the *Monthly*, and has bought a copy of *Evelina*. He has been much affected by the *Ode*, and is reading the book to Lady Hales and another friend. He thinks the Preface and Dedication "*vastly strong and well written*," Susan reports to the author. The account of public places (he declares) is "very animated, and natural, and not *common*"; and in his opinion, Lowndes has had a very good bargain. By June 16 he has finished it. It is "the best novel he knows," says the proud father, "excepting Fielding's," and in some respects it is better even than his. His only objection is to Mirvan's treatment of Lovel, which is "a brutality which does not make one laugh." Villars and Lord Orville he admired greatly; and he has "blubbered" over the scenes at the end between Evelina and Sir John Belmont. As to his lady auditors, they are still crying. For Fanny's sake

("Poor Fan's *such* a prude"), he will keep the secret snug; but he evidently does not apprehend that its disclosure would bring her any discredit. "For a young woman's work, I look upon it to be really WONDERFUL!"

All this Susan Burney recapitulates with abundant decorative detail to the delighted author at Chessington, whose foremost anxiety had been as to her father's opinion. She herself has been reading the book aloud to Mr. Crisp, who, good, easy man, has no suspicions, but is interested, and tantalised into greater curiosity by having to wait patiently for the successive volumes. Presently *Evelina* is recommended by a lady to Mrs. Thrale, who "likes it VASTLY — is EXTREMELY pleased with it." Whatever human *nature* there may be in Mme. Riccoboni,[1] she tells Mrs. Burney, who has been praising that writer, there is human *life* in *Evelina*, and the manners of the time. "It's writ (she says) by somebody that knows *the top and the bottom*, the *highest* and *lowest* of mankind." Thereupon Mrs. Burney borrows it to read; and long letters go off to Fanny embodying the remarks of both parents over the book as they study it slowly in bed in the morning. Finally, as Dr. Burney has obtained Fanny's leave to tell Mrs. Thrale, Mrs. Burney also has to be told. And then — crown of all things! — comes a congratulatory letter from Mrs. Thrale herself, praising *Evelina* for "probability of story, elegance of sentiment, and

---

[1] Marie-Jeanne de Heurles de Laboras, Mme. Riccoboni, *d.* 1792, translated Fielding's *Amelia* and Kelly's *False Delicacy* into French, and continued Marivaux's *Marianne*. She wrote several sentimental novels, one of which Mrs. Brooke Englished as *Lady Catesby's Letters.*

general power over the mind, whether exerted in humour or pathos." But "the cream of the correspondence," as Tony Lumpkin calls it, is not for once in a postscript. It is in the middle. Dr. JOHNSON has read the first two volumes, and protests there are "passages in the book which might do honour to Richardson." He is hungering for the *dénoûment*, and is now hard at work on volume three. This astounding intelligence has such an effect upon the author that, in her own words, "it almost crazed her with agreeable surprise." It gave her such a flight of spirits that she then and there "danced a jigg to Mr. Crisp, without any preparation, music, or explanation, — to his no small amazement, and diversion." She was an expert emulator of the light-heeled Nancy Dawson; and the scene of this impromptu performance — as she told Sir Walter Scott forty-eight years afterwards — was a mulberry tree in the garden at Chessington.[1]

"Daddy" Crisp was now almost the only person out of the secret; and he had to be enlightened. Dr. Burney took this duty upon himself when he came down to Chessington in August to fetch away his daughter; and the old man's pride and surprise and delight were unbounded.

[1] *Journal of Sir Walter Scott*, 1891, i. 309.

CHAPTER IV

THE SUCCESSFUL AUTHOR

ONCE — so runs the story — when Miss Burney was dining with Sir Joshua Reynolds at that pleasant villa upon Richmond Hill which had been built for him by Chambers the architect, she chanced to see him looking at her in a peculiar way. "I know what you are thinking about," — she said. "Ay," he replied, "you may come and sit to me now whenever you please." He had at last caught her special attitude, — her distinctive phase. "I hope he will take your picture," "Daddy" Crisp had said, when she first made the artist's acquaintance; — "who knows, but the time may come when your image may appear . . . like Garrick with the Comic and Tragic Muse contending for you?" Thalia and Melpomene were certainly to contend for the author of *Evelina,* and that at no distant date. There is however no picture of Fanny Burney in the Reynolds Gallery. Hoppner painted her later; but Hoppner is not Sir Joshua. Her best likeness, one of two from the same hand, is by her cousin, Edward Burney, who, it is hinted, surveyed his model —

"in the light
Of tender personal regards," —

and — it is also hinted — possibly slightly flattered her.

Edward Burney's portrait, which is prefixed to the *Diary and Letters* of 1842–6, had been mezzotinted two years earlier by Charles Turner on a larger scale. It is said to represent Miss Burney at the age of thirty, having been painted at Chessington in August 1782. She wears a hat and feathers ; and her hair is frizzed out in the approved fashion of the day. Her attitude is conventional :— she sits demurely erect, with formally posed hands. But her eyes are brimming with latent animation ; and the corners of the lips are lifted with a lurking sense of fun. Of the sitter's stature the picture gives little indication. She is reported, however, to have been extremely slight and frail of make — "a small cargo for the Chessington coach," said Mr. Crisp. It was perhaps owing to this that she preserved so long her youthful and almost girlish appearance. As to her eyes, which, in the portrait, look large and luminous, we have her own assurance that they were greenish gray ; and from the fact that she was called "the dove" by one of her Tunbridge friends, we must assume that they resembled those of Mrs. Delany, who is praised by her adoring husband for "what Solomon calls 'dove's eyes.'" Her complexion was brown; and she is affirmed to have been rather French-looking. Beautiful of feature, perhaps, she could scarcely be called. But it is admitted that she had great charm of expression, and a countenance which was quick to betray every passing emotion. "Poor Fanny's face" — said her father — "tells us what she thinks whether she will or no"; and she confirms this herself by lamenting her lack of power to command her features. She "rouged" readily — to use her own euphemism for blushing. For the rest, she was all her life ailing and delicate. But like many valetudinarians, she succeeded in surviving her robuster relatives. She out-lasted all her sisters except one; and she lived to the age of eighty-seven.[1]

When Dr. Burney fetched his daughter from Chessington, it had been arranged that they should stop at Streatham Place on their way back to town. This they did; and Fanny's diary gives a full account of what she pronounces to be "the most consequential day she had spent since her birth." Mrs. Thrale was very gracious, and very discreet, only mentioning *Evelina* in order to refer to Dr. Johnson's genuine admiration for the book. Mr. Seward, whom we remember as one of the visitors to St. Martin's Street, was not by any means so considerate, bluntly blurting out his praises in the most embarrassing manner. At dinner a place was left next Miss Burney for Dr. Johnson, who presently appeared. The Doctor was as delicate as Mrs. Thrale, only touching indirectly and circuitously upon the burning topic. Asked by Mrs. Thrale to have some little pies of mutton, he declared gallantly that sitting next Miss Burney made him too proud to eat mutton. Later, after some rambling talk about the wear and tear of Garrick's face, he went on to

---

[1] Edward Francis Burney, 1760–1848, the artist referred to in the above paragraph, was a frequent contributor to the Royal Academy between 1780 and 1793. His solitary "Portrait of a Lady," 1785, *may* have been his cousin's picture. His first exhibits (418–20) were three "stained Drawings" for *Evelina*, in which Mme. Duval, Captain Mirvan, Mr. Villars, the heroine and her father, were all introduced. The Evelina of these designs is said to have strongly resembled the beautiful Sophy Streatfield ; and an artful compliment was paid to Johnson by hanging his portrait in Mr. Villars' parlour. Archdeacon Burney has one of these delicate little pictures.

speak of Dr. Burney's rival, Sir John Hawkins, whom he can scarcely be said to have extolled. He believed him "an honest man at the bottom; but to be sure," he continued, "he is penurious, and he is mean, and it must be owned he has a degree of brutality, and a tendency to savageness, that cannot easily be defended." Giving an instance of Sir John's "*unclubbable*" character, he added that it reminded him of a lady with whom he had once travelled, who, stopping at an inn in her own coach and four, called for — a pint of ale! quarrelling moreover with the waiter for not giving full measure. And here came in another adroit allusion to *Evelina*. "Mme. Duval"— said the Doctor —"could not have done a grosser thing!"—a sentiment which of course convulsed the company, and threw the young person at his side into the most delicious confusion. Altogether the visit was delightful; and when Fanny and her father got into the chaise to go, it was a settled thing that she was to come again to Streatham, and for a much longer stay.

When she reached St. Martin's Street, there were further honours in store for her. Hetty had lately met Frances Reynolds, who was full of the new novel, "though without a shadow of suspicion as to the scribbler." This, of itself, was not much; but Miss Reynolds also announced that her brother, Sir Joshua, having begun it when "he was too much engaged to go on with it, was so much caught, that he could think of nothing else, and was quite absent all the day, not knowing a word that was said to him; and, when he took it up again, found himself so much interested in it, that he sat up all night to finish it!" He would give fifty pounds, he had subsequently declared, to know the author, and other people were equally inquisitive. After this astounding piece of intelligence, Fanny thought she would herself go to Mr. Thomas Lowndes, and ascertain in what way that gentleman was satisfying the eagerness of enquirers. As she could not trust herself to speak, her step-mother went with her. They began by buying a copy, and then asked Mr. Lowndes — a pompous and consequential personage who happened to be in the shop — if he could tell them who wrote it. No, he replied, he did not know himself. Pressed further, he said that the author was a gentleman of the other end of the town; and, in response to renewed cross-questioning on Mrs. Burney's part, affirmed that he was a master of his subject, and well versed in the manners of the times. Moreover, that he (Mr. Lowndes) had at first thought *Evelina* was by Horace Walpole, who had once published a book in the same "snug manner,"[1] but he did not think so now. (Other people, it may be noted, had attributed it to Christopher Anstey of the *New Bath Guide*, then some dozen years old, — a work which Miss Anville and Lord Orville peruse together at Mrs. Beaumont's.) Finally, out of sheer inability to satisfy his interrogator, Mr. Lowndes hinted darkly, "with a most important face," that he had been told that the authorship of *Evelina* was a piece of real secret history, which could consequently never be known. This final piece of information was too much for the listener, who "was obliged to look out at the shop-door" for the remainder of the interview. To the modern student Fanny's investigations would have been more satisfying

---

[1] No doubt *The Castle of Otranto*, which Lowndes himself had published in 1764.

if they had thrown some definite light on the progress of the book from the publisher's point of view. In spite of various statements to the contrary, it seems clear that when, in August, 1778, she and her step-mother went to Fleet Street, Mr. Lowndes was still selling the first impression. The second edition is dated 1779; and in October, 1796, the author wrote that "the first edition of *Evelina* was of eight hundred, the second of five hundred, and the third of a thousand" copies. On the other hand, Lowndes, who should certainly have been acquainted with the facts, informed Dr. Burney, in an unpublished letter of 1782, that he only printed a first edition of five hundred. Whichever be the correct version of the story, it is pretty clear that the sale for the first twelve months can scarcely be regarded as extraordinary.[1]

[1] The bibliography of Miss Burney's first book is extremely perplexing. In the "Advertisement" to *Cecilia*, the author says that *Evelina* (which, it will be remembered, appeared in January, 1778) passed "through Four Editions in one year." In the *Memoirs of Dr. Burney*, she implies that it went through three editions in five months (ii. p. 135). But the second and third editions are both dated 1779; and it must have been in the first months of that year that the sale was most active. In May, 1779, comes a reference to the fourth edition as on the stocks. "*Evelina* continues to sell in a most wonderful manner; a fourth edition is preparing, with cuts [it should be copper plates], designed by Mortimer just before he died, and executed by Hall and Bartolozzi" (*Diary and Letters*, 1892, i. p. 139). John Hamilton Mortimer, A.R.A., the artist indicated, died 4th February, 1779. His drawings, which cost £73, still exist. It may here be added that Mrs. Chappel, of East Orchard, Shaftesbury, possesses a copy of the second edition of *Evelina* (1779), presented to Dr. Burney, — whose name is filled up in the heading of the dedicatory verses, — "From his dutiful scribler," *i.e.* "F. B."

Before the end of August Mrs. Thrale called at St. Martin's Street, and carried off her new friend to Streatham Place; and at Streatham Place Fanny practically remained for the rest of 1778. The inviting white house with its wooded park, or enclosure, where—to use Susan Burney's expression—the "cattle, poultry, and dogs all ran freely about without annoying each other," has now long been a thing of the past, having been pulled down in 1863. Its site was the southern side of the lower common between Streatham and Tooting. It was a three-storied building, with many cheerful rooms which Fanny's records make familiar to us. The saloon was hung with sky blue; and there was a parlour for the more crowded dinner parties, decorated with prints by Hogarth and others which, probably inaccurately, are described as being "pasted" on the walls. The library, also used frequently as a breakfast room, had been built by Mr. Thrale about 1773, and was kept stocked with books by Johnson, who here — said Mrs. Thrale — "talked Ramblers," while she read aloud the last proofs of the *Lives of the Poets*. Above the book-cases, hung the famous Thrale Gallery, dispersed in 1816, — portraits by Sir Joshua of Johnson, of Burke, of the artist himself, of Goldsmith, Garrick, Murphy, Baretti, Dr. Burney and other visitors to the house. Over the fireplace, and also by Reynolds, was the double picture of Mrs. Thrale and Queenie, which was exhibited in the Grosvenor Gallery in 1884. In the grounds, besides plantations, and high-walled kitchen gardens with ice-houses and pineries, there was an encircling shrubbery which bordered a gravelled walk of nearly two miles. There was also a spring pond, dug by

Thrale, which, apparently in imitation of Duck Island in St. James's Park, boasted its Dick's Island; and there was "a cool summer-house," where Johnson wrote and studied, and Fanny read, or essayed to read, *Irene*. It must have been a most delightful country-house, meriting fully the Doctor's grateful eulogy that "none but itself could be its parallel." "I have found nothing," he wrote from Lichfield in 1767, "that withdraws my affections from the friends whom I left behind, or which makes me less desirous of reposing at that place which your kindness and Mr. Thrale's allows me to call my *home*." "These are as good people," he said to Miss Burney in the first days of her visit, "as you can be with; you can go to no better house; they are all good nature; nothing makes them angry."

He himself seems to have softened with his environment. Although, as Fanny says, the freedom with which he condemned what he disapproved was astonishing, and his strength of language would to most persons be intolerable, he presented, upon the whole, a far more benignant aspect than that in which he is usually exhibited by Boswell. He is Johnson in clover, and *en belle humeur;* happier and more at ease than he is elsewhere, and therefore more agreeable. To the yet undisclosed author of *Evelina* he is especially gracious, and even affectionate. He kisses her hand; makes her sit by him; pays her elaborate compliments; and no one, when he pleased, could do that better. "Harry Fielding," he protested, "never drew so good a character" as her Mr. Smith. "Such a fine varnish of low politeness! — such a struggle to appear a gentleman! Madam [to Mrs. Thrale], there is no

character better drawn anywhere — in any book, or by
any author" — an extravagance which almost leads one
particular author present to "poke herself under the
table." He bursts out with sudden quotations from
Evelina: — with Miss Branghton's "Only think, Polly!
Miss has danced with a Lord!" — he rallies poor Mr.
Seward on his resemblance to the Holborn beau. —
"Why, you only want a tambour waistcoat, to look
like Mr. Smith!" Then he is heard grumbling to
himself over a letter from Fanny's medical adviser,
Dr. Jebb, whose penmanship is that of a tradesman.
"Mr. Branghton would have written his name with
just such beastly flourishes!" But perhaps the acme
of his amiable speeches is his frank comparison of
"dear little Burney," as he comes to call her, with
Fielding and Richardson. "Richardson," he said,
"would have been really afraid of her; there is
merit," he went on, "in *Evelina* which he could not
have borne. No; it would not have done! unless,
indeed, she would have flattered him prodigiously.
Harry Fielding, too, would have been afraid of her;
there is nothing so delicately finished in all Harry
Fielding's works as in *Evelina*." Then, shaking his
head at her, he exclaimed, "O, you little character-
monger you!" — an appellation which must be admitted to be singularly appropriate. On another
occasion, he declared that she was his "hero." "Dr.
Goldsmith was my last; but I have had none since his
time, till my little Burney came."[1]   "I admire her"

---

[1] This phrase of "Little Burney" — or more generally "dear
little Burney" — to the sensitive Fanny's "infinite *frettation*"
got into print. A certain Rev. George Huddesford embodied it
in a rhymed satire upon the camp which fears of French invasion

— he said again, and to her face — "for her observation, for her good sense, for her humour, for her dis-
cernment, for her manner of expressing them, and for
all her writing talents." Decidedly it was good to be
praised by Johnson; and one may well forgive Miss
Burney for doubting whether she could possibly live
up to his laudation.

Visitors to Streatham Place came and went so freely
that it is difficult to chronicle them. Among the rest
was that accomplished *esprit fort*, Mrs. Elizabeth
Montagu, to whom Mrs. Thrale could not deny herself the pleasure of exhibiting her own special prize
and discovery, the author of *Evelina*. Mrs. Montagu
came to Streatham by invitation, accompanied by her
friend, Miss Gregory. Dr. Johnson was very anxious
that "Burney" should attack the "Queen of the Blue
Stockings," much as, in his own hot youth, he had
hawked at all established wits. But Mrs. Thrale,
finding that Mrs. Montagu knew nothing of *Evelina*,
disclosed the secret of the authorship so abruptly,
that Fanny fairly took to her heels and fled. Hence
she saw less of the great lady than she would otherwise; and between the extreme blame of "Daddy"
Crisp and the extreme praise of Mrs. Thrale, was
not perhaps greatly prepossessed in favour of Mrs.
Montagu, who, moreover, had been so ill-advised as
never to have heard of *Evelina*. But Mrs. Montagu
was very well-bred and polite; and easily fell in with
Dr. Johnson's suggestion that Miss Burney should

had established at Warley Common in Essex, and which King
George and Queen Charlotte visited in October, 1788. Johnson
had gone there earlier, as the guest of Bennet Langton, who was a
Captain in the Lincolnshire militia.

H

accompany the rest of those present to the house-warming with which she hoped shortly to open her new abode in Portman Square, — that famous mansion of the feather-hangings celebrated by Cowper's —

> " The Birds put off their every hue
> To dress a room for Montagu."

It was in reference to a suggestion by Mrs. Montagu that Fanny's dedication was good enough to have been written by her father — a suggestion which, with all her filial affection, Fanny could scarcely be expected to welcome very warmly — that Johnson uttered one of his common-sense deliverances on criticism. " You must not mind that" — he said to Mrs. Montagu's impolitic remark, — "for such things are always said where books are successful. There are three distinct kinds of judges upon all new authors or productions; the first are those who know no rules, but pronounce entirely from their natural taste and feelings ; the second are those who know and judge by rules; and the third are those who know, but are above the rules. These last are those you should wish to satisfy. Next to them rate the natural judges; but ever despise those opinions that are formed by the rules." Of this second class, his own " Dick Minim " is an admirable exemplification.[1]

In January, 1779, Miss Burney was again at St. Martin's Street, her sister Susan being from home. St. Martin's Street has a mysterious visit from "a square old gentleman, well-wigged, formal, grave and important," who suddenly asks her if she is not *Evelina*, and turns out to be Dr. Francklin, chaplain

[1] *Idler*, June 9 and 16, 1759.

to the Royal Academy. Then she is invited to
Sir Joshua's to meet Mrs. and Miss [Mary] Horneck
(Goldsmith's "Jessamy Bride"), soon to be married
to Colonel Gwyn. The ladies had said that they
would walk a hundred and sixty miles to see her, so
there was nothing to excuse her for not stepping
across the Fields to No. 47. Here she met another
admirer, Peg Woffington's witty and eccentric sister,
Mrs. Cholmondeley; and Lord Palmerston, father of
the Victorian premier; and Burke's brother William,
the "honest William" of Goldsmith's *Retaliation*. All,
and especially Sir Joshua, were most cordial, though
Mrs. Cholmondeley's "pointed speeches," Duval *Ma
foi's*, and references to *Evelina* generally, would have
been embarrassing, even to a less nervous person
than the author. Mrs. Cholmondeley, among other
things, had been to Lowndes for information, getting
nothing from that windbag but intelligence that a
gentleman had betted that the writer of *Evelina* was
a man, while she, Mrs. Cholmondeley, felt equally convinced it was a woman. " But now " — she added —
" we are both out; for it's a girl! " — which must be
accepted as unanswerable testimony to Fanny's youthful appearance at six-and-twenty.

This interview with Mrs. Cholmondeley, who had
been one of the book's earliest and most energetic
trumpeters (it was she, indeed, who had first recommended it " among the wits "), was of course followed
by an invitation, which proved a most important one.
For at Mrs. Cholmondeley's in Hertford Street she
met, not only the beautiful " St. Cecilia " of Reynolds,
with her almost equally beautiful sister, Miss Linley ;
but she met " St. Cecilia's " husband, the all-conquering

author of the recently-produced *School for Scandal* and
manager of Drury Lane, Richard Brinsley Sheridan
himself, of whom she writes admiringly. He has
" a good though I don't think a handsome face. He
is tall, and very upright, and his appearance and
address are at once manly and fashionable, without
the smallest tincture of foppery or modish graces. In
short, I like him vastly, and think him every way
worthy his beautiful companion," — to whom, Fanny
adds, he was manifestly much devoted. By and by,
Sheridan introduced himself to Miss Burney, and was
most agreeable. He had been telling her father, he
said, that he had long expected to see in her " a lady
of the gravest appearance, with the quickest parts."
He expressed the highest admiration for *Evelina*,
adding that he hoped she (Miss Burney) did not
intend to throw away her pen. He was very curious
to know what she was about, and Sir Joshua observed
that she must succeed in "anything in the dialogue
way." Mr. Sheridan assented. He thought "she
should write a comedy." "And you," said the
. kind Sir Joshua presently, "would take anything of
hers, would you not? — unsight, unseen?" "Yes," he
answered with quickness, "and make her a bow and
my best thanks into the bargain." Here was a piece
of news to post off to Susan !

As a matter of fact, Miss Burney was already
engaged upon a dramatic essay. Both her father
and " Daddy " Crisp were anxious that, before interest
cooled, she should follow up her first success by some
other work ; and from the date of Mrs. Thrale's first
letter to Dr. Burney,[1] that lady had been pressing her

[1] See *ante*, p. 86.

to write for the stage.   She had the same conviction
as Reynolds that something "in the dialogue way"
would suit her young friend.   *Evelina* — Mrs. Thrale
thought — ran so naturally into conversations that it
absolutely and plainly pointed that path to her.   If
she could not do better than Hannah More, who got
nearly four hundred pounds for her foolish play,[1] she
deserved to be whipped — said this kindly enthusiast.
Dr. Johnson, after see-sawing immoderately, proposed,
in a fit of untimely levity, that her first work should
be entitled, *Streatham: A Farce;* but he, too, heartily approved.   Mrs. Montagu, who was consulted,
though she was sympathetic, was not so sure.   She
advanced the case of Fielding, who failed upon the
stage.   And "Daddy" Crisp was still more half-
hearted.   He wrote to Fanny an admirable letter
upon the subject.   While he was urgent that she
should do something, he was by no means satisfied
that the something in question should be a comedy.
In a second letter he developed his ideas.   She had
gained much: she had much to lose.   And play-
writing — for her — had its peculiar difficulties.   Her
delicacy (and she was a prude, she knew herself)
would debar her from those frequent lively freedoms
without which comedy would lose wonderfully of its
salt and spirit.   All the same he would evidently
not have her try the bloodless and prevalent sentimental comedy.   About Fielding, he agreed with
Mrs. Montagu.   Finally, though he did not wholly
desire to discourage her from the attempt, he thought
that, in entering upon it, she must surrender a part

[1] Miss Hannah More's successful tragedy of *Percy* was produced
at Covent Garden, 10 December, 1777.

of her strength. And here we may use his actual
words: — " In these little entertaining elegant histories
[such as *Evelina*], the writer has his full scope; as
large a range as he pleases to hunt in — to pick, cull,
select whatever he likes: he takes his own time — he
may be as minute as he pleases, and the more minute
the better, provided that taste, a deep and penetrating
knowledge of human nature and the world, accompany
that minuteness. When this is the case, the very soul,
and all its most secret recesses and workings, are
developed and laid as open to the view, as the blood-
globules circulating in a frog's foot, when seen through
a microscope. The exquisite touches such a work is
capable of (of which *Evelina* is, without flattery, a
glaring instance), are truly charming. But of these
great advantages, these resources, you are strangely
curtailed the moment you begin a comedy. There,
everything passes in dialogue, — all goes on rapidly —
narrative and descriptive, if not extremely short,
becomes intolerable. The detail which in Fielding,
Marivaux, and Crébillon, is so delightful, on the stage
would bear down all patience. There all must be
compressed into quintessence; the moment the scene
ceases to move on briskly, and business seems to
hang, sighs and groans are the consequence. Dreadful sound! — In a word, if the plot, the story of the
comedy, does not open and unfold itself in the easy,
natural, unconstrained flow of the dialogue — if that
dialogue does not go on with spirit, wit, variety, fun,
humour, repartee, — and all in short into the bargain
— *serviteur!* — good-bye t' ye ! "

This is excellently said, and shows once again how
precept may excel practice, — though, to be sure,

"Daddy" Crisp's *Virginia* was a tragedy, and not a
comedy. In a later letter Fanny's Mentor modified
his views to the extent of admitting that it was possible, with due contrivance and dexterity, to display
light principles without light expressions; but he stuck
to the proposition that he would never allow his Fannikin "to sacrifice a grain of female delicacy for all
the wit of Congreve and Vanbrugh put together," —
and in this she was entirely of his mind. These
letters preceded the interview with Sheridan; and as
we have already said, she had probably begun to work
on a comedy still earlier.[1] When, in February, she
got back to Streatham, she made the acquaintance
of Arthur Murphy, in whose *Way to Keep Him* she
had acted at Barborne Lodge. He, too, volunteered
the suggestion that she should write for the stage.
Comedy, in his opinion, was the forte of *Evelina*, and
he offered his skilled assistance. He subsequently gave
her some rules by which she was too far advanced in
her work to profit — rules which, Johnson consolingly
told her, she would do just as well without. In May
her play is finished, though "on account of the various
Maecenases who would expect to be consulted," the
greatest secrecy is observed. Murphy applauds; and
so does Mrs. Thrale. Johnson apparently was not
consulted. But when it is carried off by Dr. Burney
to "Daddy" Crisp, the verdict of Fanny's "highest
court" is unfavourable. Indeed, in what she calls a
"hissing, groaning, cat-calling epistle," they go as far
as to recommend its suppression. Not only did it
recall the *Femmes Savantes* of Molière (which Fanny
had never read), but they regarded the plot and

[1] See *Diary and Letters*, 1892, i. p. 48.

incidents as insufficient to hold the attention of the audience. Fanny took her disappointment bravely, and at once threw her work aside. Later on, when it became necessary to explain matters to Sheridan, there was some talk of remodelling, and with this object the fourth act was almost entirely re-written. But Crisp, who was appealed to, stood to his guns. He thought the capital defect of an ill-planned fable beyond remedy, though he admitted the wit of the play.

Here the matter seems to have rested; and all we know of the suppressed piece is, that it was entitled *The Witlings*, and that the *dramatis personae* included, among others, a quotation-loving Lady Smatter (in whom Mrs. Thrale professed to recognise her own portrait), Mrs. Voluble, Mrs. Wheedle, Mrs. Sapient, Dabbler, Censor, and a "great oaf, Bobby." There was also — and the point is memorable in view of the title of Miss Burney's next novel — a Cecilia, the loss and restoration of whose fortune were matters in debate. Whether Dr. Burney and his friend were right in their judgment of *The Witlings*, cannot now be affirmed or denied in the absence of the MS. Probably they were right; though they do not seem to have borne in mind how material a part the acting bears in the success of a piece; and at Sheridan's theatre, Miss Burney's comedy would certainly have been splendidly represented. King, Dodd, Palmer, Parsons, Mrs. Abington, and Miss Pope — would all probably have taken part in it. But Fanny's advisers, it is clear, were also actuated by another reflection, of which Murphy knew nothing: they feared the effect upon the author of a possible *fiasco*. "My great scruple all along has been the consideration of the great stake

you are playing for," — writes Mr. Crisp, — " how much
you have to lose, and how unequal your delicate and
tender frame of mind would be to sustain the shock of
a failure of success, should that be the case." This is
perhaps not a critical reason; but, at the same time,
it is a reason beyond criticism. And " Daddy " Crisp
shows plainly that it was *The Witlings* he doubted, —
not Fanny's ability to produce comedy. For, in an
earlier letter, he had suggested to her a fresh effort,
based upon certain of her own experiences as narrated
to her father.

It was early in 1779 that Miss Burney made the
acquaintance of Sheridan at Mrs. Cholmondeley's; and
it was not until the beginning of 1780 that *The
Witlings* was practically abandoned. In the interim,
at Streatham and elsewhere, Fanny seems to have
spent her time very agreeably. In May, she went
with the Thrales to Brighton, returning, apparently,
early in June, owing to the sudden illness of Mr.
Thrale. But in October they were again at Brighton,
taking Knole Park (Lord Dorset's) and its magnificent
galleries in their way, and making a short stay at
Tunbridge Wells, where Miss Burney pours scorn upon
the famous Pantiles as a fashionable pleasure walk.
" It has no beauty in itself, and borrows none from
foreign aid, as it has only common houses at one side,
and little millinery and Tunbridge-ware shops at the
other, and at each end is choked up by buildings that
intercept all prospect." At Brighton, no doubt in the
interests of *Evelina*, Mrs. Thrale at once inscribed their
names at the booksellers' shops upon the Steyne. At
this date there were no great notabilities at Bright-
helmstone, as Fanny styles the place, save " that cele-

brated wit and libertine," the Hon. Mr. Beauclerk, and his wife, Lady Di; Cumberland the dramatist and his family; and Mrs. Musters, whose son married Byron's first love, Mary Chaworth. The Miss Cumberlands were reckoned "the flashers of the place," and Fanny gives an account of their father which reads like a scene from the *Critic*. "Sir Fretful Plagiary" was already prejudiced against her on account of her success; and when he called on Mrs. Thrale, he showed it. As soon as she had quitted the room he said to Mrs. Thrale, "with a spiteful tone of voice,

"'Oh, that young lady is an author, I hear!'

"'Yes,' answered Mrs. Thrale, 'author of *Evelina*.'

"'Humph — I am told it has some humour!'

"'Ay, indeed! Johnson says nothing like it has appeared for years!'

"'So,' cried he, biting his lips, and waving uneasily in his chair, 'so, so!'

"'Yes,' continued she; 'and Sir Joshua Reynolds told Mr. Thrale he would give fifty pounds to know the author!'

"'So, so — oh, vastly well!' cried he, putting his hand on his forehead.

"'Nay!' added she, 'Burke himself sat up all night to finish it!'

"This seemed quite too much for him; he put both his hands to his face, and waving backwards and forwards, said, 'Oh, vastly well! — this will do for anything!' with a tone as much as to say, Pray, no more! Then Mrs. Thrale bid him good night, longing, she said, to call Miss Thrale first, and say, 'So you won't speak to my daughter? — why, she is no author.'"

Some of the persons sketched in Miss Burney's

journal are less known to fame than those who have
been mentioned, but they are not less cleverly drawn.
There is Mr. Seward, one of the Streatham *habitués*,
and the later author of *Biographiana*. Mr. Seward is
a brewer's son, who dabbles in letters, and seems like
an earlier real-life version of Sir Charles Coldstream in
Used Up. With " Mr. Dry," as Miss Burney calls him,
she playfully proposes to collaborate in a comedy, to
be entitled *Everything a Bore*. There is a real tragic
author, Dr. John Delap, who, while as absent-minded
and as ignorant of the world as Parson Adams, is
engaged upon a play called *Macaria*,[1] on the story of
the wife and daughter of Hercules, which Fanny has
to read and criticise — or rather eulogise. There is a
very musical, precocious, and semi-French ten-year-old
schoolgirl, Miss Birch, who sings sentimental airs from
French operas, and says to her friends, " *Que je vous
adore!*"—"*Ah, permettez que je me mette à vos pieds!*"
etc., with a dying languor that is equally delightful
and preposterous. And there is that finished and
fascinating coquette of coquettes, Miss Sophy Streatfield of Tunbridge Wells, who knows Greek as well as
Miss Elizabeth Carter or Mrs. Buller, is as lovely as
Mrs. Crewe or Mrs. Sheridan, and has moreover a
faculty for shedding tears so becoming to her lackadaisical cast of beauty that she is periodically required (like the water works at Vauxhall) to display
her unique gift for the public delectation. Fanny's
description of Miss Streatfield's mechanical *grandes eaux*
is too good to be neglected. We must imagine her

[1] Probably that afterwards produced at Drury Lane in 1781
as *The Royal Suppliants*, and based upon the *Heraclidæ* of
Euripides.

surrounded by attentive spectators, with Mrs. Thrale
(like Mrs. Jarley) for exhibitor. " 'Yes, do cry a
little, Sophy [*in a wheedling voice*], pray, do! Consider,
now, you are going to-day, and it's very hard if you
won't cry a little; indeed, S. S., you ought to cry.'
Now for the wonder of wonders. When Mrs. Thrale,
in a coaxing voice, suited to a nurse soothing a baby,
had run on for some time — while all the rest of us, in
laughter, joined in the request — two crystal tears came
into the soft eyes of the S. S., and rolled gently down
her cheeks! Such a sight I never saw before, nor could
I have believed.[1] She offered not to conceal or dis-
sipate them : on the contrary, she really contrived to
have them seen by everybody. She looked, indeed,
uncommonly handsome, for her pretty face was not
like Chloe's [in Prior], blubbered; it was smooth and
elegant, and neither her features nor complexion were
at all ruffled; nay, indeed, she was smiling all the
time." It is melancholy to think that a lady who
possessed in such perfection the attributes of Venus
Victrix, should die unmarried. Yet this was the
untoward fate of the "S. S." "Everybody's admiration, and nobody's choice," as one of her friends said,
she survived until 1835, an ancient maiden lady, concerning whom we do not even know whether — like
Pope's Patty Blount — she retained to the last the
charm of her wonderful blue eyes.

But Miss Streatfield is not the person upon whom
Miss Burney concentrates her fullest powers of
description. That honour is reserved for an uniden-

---

[1] Miss Burney here forgets that she had already assisted at a
private view of Miss Streatfield's performance (*Diary and Letters*, 1892, i. p. 135-6).

tified Mr. B—y, to whom she devotes several pages.
Mr. B—y, or " The General," as she styles him, is an
Irishman. He has been a Commissary in Germany;
is between sixty and seventy, but means to pass for
thirty; a professed admirer of the sex, whom he
invariably calls " fair females "; garnishes his speech
with French tags of the most hackneyed kind; quotes
often and inaccurately, and although Fanny, afraid
of painting too much *en noir*, declares him to be
worthy and moral at bottom, seems to outward view
to be nothing but a blundering, prejudiced, puffing,
domineering busybody and bore. He is enraged with
Reynolds for charging seventy guineas " to scratch out
a head "; he is enraged with Garrick for living like
a person of quality; he is enraged with Agujari for
getting fifty pounds for a mere song; he is equally
enraged with Rauzzini because the " fair females " sigh
over him, and make a man sick. But the General's
standing topic is his health; his rooted antipathy,
physicians; and his favourite story — which he tells
three or four times a day — in this wise: — " ' Some
years ago,' — he says — ' let's see, how many ? in the
year '71 — ay, '71, '72 — thereabouts — I was taken very
ill, and, by ill luck, I was persuaded to ask the advice
of one of these Dr. Gallipots: — oh, how I hate them
all! Sir, they are the vilest pickpockets, — know
nothing, sir! Nothing in the world! poor ignorant
mortals! and they pretend — in short, sir, I hate them
all; I have suffered so much by them, sir — lost four
years of the happiness of my life — let's see, '71, '72,
'73, '74 — ay, four years, sir! — mistook my case, sir! —
and all that kind of thing. Why, sir, my feet swelled
as big as two horses' heads! I vow I will never

consult one of these Dr. Gallipot fellows again! lost
me, sir, four years of the happiness of my life! — why,
I grew quite an object! — you would hardly have
known me! — lost all the calves of my legs! — had not
an ounce of flesh left! — and as to the rouge — why,
my face was the colour of that candle! — those Gallipot fellows! — why, they robbed me of four years —
let me see, '71, '72 — '

" And then it all goes over again!

" This story is always *a-propos* ; if health is mentioned, it is instanced to show its precariousness; if
life, to bewail what he has lost of it; if pain, to relate
what he has suffered; if pleasure, to recapitulate what
he has been deprived of; but if a physician is hinted
at, eagerly indeed is the opportunity seized of inveigh-
ing against the whole faculty."

There is more, especially of the General grumbling
over the newspaper; but enough has been given. In
all these pictures, it may be noted, Miss Burney insists
upon her fidelity to fact. " I never mix truth and
fiction," she tells " Daddy " Crisp. " I have other
purposes for imaginary characters than filling letters
with them." " The world, and especially the Great
world, is so filled with absurdity of various sorts, now
bursting forth in impertinence, now in pomposity, now
giggling in silliness, and now yawning in dullness, that
there is no occasion for invention to draw what is
striking in every possible species of the ridiculous."
As time went on, her opportunities for study rather
increased than decreased. At the beginning of 1780,
as already related, the question of her comedy was
again partly revived. Then there were proposals for
a tour in Italy with the Thrales which was afterwards

abandoned. But in April she went with her friends to Bath, making acquaintance *en route*, at the Bear at Devizes, with the hostess's clever son, who afterwards became Sir Thomas Lawrence. At Bath they lodge (like Smollett's Mr. Bramble) in the South Parade, with Allen's Prior Park, the meadows, and "the soft flowing Avon" in view; and are speedily absorbed in the fashionable diversions of the place. Prelates were preaching at the Abbey and St. James's Churches; there were public breakfasts in the Spring Gardens; the Pump Room was crowded with company and the Walks with promenaders; Mrs. Siddons was playing Belvidera at Mr. Palmer's Theatre in Orchard Street; and life was one endless round of fiddles, dinners, concerts, assemblies, balls, card-parties and scandal. Miss Burney's canvas becomes more and more crowded, and less detailed, affording space only for occasional vignettes such as the following: "In the evening we had Mrs. L——, a fat, round, panting, short-breathed old widow; and her daughter, a fubsy, good-humoured, laughing, silly, merry old maid. They are rich folks, and live together very comfortably, and the daughter sings — not in your fine Italian taste! no, that she and her mother agree to hold very cheap — but all about Daphne, and Chloe, and Damon, and Phillis, and Jockey!" Or this, — on the same page, — "Mrs. K—— is a Welsh lady, of immense fortune, who has a house in the Crescent, and lives in a most magnificent style. She is about fifty, very good-humoured, well-bred, and civil, and her waist does not measure above a hogshead. She is not very deep, I must own; but what of that? If all were wits, where would be the admirers at them?"

Dr. Johnson did not take part in the Bath expedition. He would, indeed, have come; but Mrs. Thrale had discouraged his doing so, feeling sure that a watering-place life would have horribly wearied him, which is not only possible but extremely probable. Literature — that is to say the literature of 1780 — was nevertheless fairly represented in Bladud's ancient City. First and foremost there was Mrs. Thrale's rival, Mrs. Montagu, with her attendant train of blue-stockings; there was Anstey of the *New Bath Guide,* whom — as we have seen — wiseacres had credited with *Evelina;* there was Mrs. Susannah Dobson, the translator of *Petrarch;* there was Melmoth of Pliny's *Letters;* there was Miss Elizabeth Carter of Epictetus; there was Lady Miller of Batheaston and the famous Frascati vase wherein — according to Macaulay — "fools were wont to put bad verses," but which, however, at this precise moment of time, was not *en fonction.*[1] To the failings of her *confrères* and *consœurs,* Miss Burney, it must be confessed, in her capacity of "faithful historian" is not always "very kind." Of poor Lady Miller, who died a year later, she writes, "She is a round, plump, coarse-looking dame of about forty, and while all her aim is to appear an elegant woman of fashion, all her success is to seem an ordinary woman in very common life, with fine clothes on. Her habits are bustling, her air is mock-important, and her

---

[1] There is an account of the Batheaston Thursday Parnassus in a letter from Walpole to Conway, 15 January, 1775. The historical urn no longer exists. But the verses cannot have been all bad. Garrick was responsible for some of them, and Graves of *The Spiritual Quixote.* Another contributor was Anstey, who wrote his *Election Ball* for Lady Miller.

manners very inelegant." Of Mrs. Dobson, she reports that "though coarse, low-bred, forward, self-sufficient, and flaunting, she seems to have a strong and masculine understanding, and parts that, had they been united with modesty, or fostered by education, might have made her a shining and agreeable woman; but she has evidently kept low company, which she has risen above in literature, but not in manners." Of Miss Carter, on the contrary, then very old, Miss Burney says, that she "never saw age so graceful in the female sex yet, her whole face seems to beam with goodness, piety and philanthropy." Anstey she finds not very agreeable — "shyly important, and silently proud," and moreover unable to forget that he is the author of a popular work; while *Pliny* Melmoth is written down as "intolerably self-sufficient."

Some of the Bath visitors were naval officers who — it should be observed — did not at all accept Captain Mirvan's portrait as typical of their profession. One of them, Mrs. Thrale's cousin, Captain Cotton, pretended "in a comical and good-humoured way" to resent it highly; and so — he told the author — did all the Captains in the Navy. Admiral Byron, too, — the Byron of the "narrative" in *Don Juan*, — though he admired *Evelina*, was "not half pleased with the Captain's being such a brute." But Miss Burney herself is unconvinced and impenitent. " The more I see of sea-captains, the less reason I have to be ashamed of Captain Mirvan; for they have all so irresistible a propensity to wanton mischief, — to roasting beaux, and detesting old women, that I quite rejoice I showed the book to no one ere printed, lest I should have been prevailed upon to soften his character." What the

I

sea-captains, and the Bathonians generally thought of their critic, is not related, save in a sentence from *Thraliana:*—" Miss Burney was much admired at Bath (1780); the puppy-men said, 'She had such a drooping air and such a timid intelligence'; or 'a timid air,' I think it was, and 'a drooping intelligence'; never sure was such a collection of pedantry and affectation as filled Bath when we were on that spot." The almost imperceptible feline touch in this passage serves to remind us that, in the padlocked privacy of her personal records, Mrs. Thrale did not scruple (like Dr. Johnson) to mingle praise with blame when occasion required. From other entries in *Thraliana,* Fanny seems to have sometimes vexed her friend by her prudish punctiliousness and dread of patronage, as well as by her perhaps more defensible preference for her own family. " What a blockhead Dr. Burney is to be always sending for his daughter home so! what a monkey! is she not better and happier with me than she can be anywhere else ? " . . . " If I did not provide Fanny with every wearable—every wishable, indeed— it would not vex me to be served so; but to see the impossibility of compensating for the pleasures of St. Martin's Street, makes one at once merry and morti- fied." There were other reasons, as we shall learn presently, why Dr. Burney was anxious that Fanny should come back.[1]

Meanwhile, early in June, the Bath visit came to a premature conclusion. Returning from a visit to Lady Miller, Mrs. Thrale received intelligence of the

[1] *Autobiography, etc., of Mrs. Piozzi (Thrale),* by A. Hayward, 1861 (2nd edn.), i. pp. 125, 126.

Gordon riots. Her house in the Borough had been besieged by the mob, and only saved from destruction by the assistance of the Guards and the presence of mind of the superintendent, Mr. Perkins. Streatham Place was also threatened, and emptied of its furniture. What was worse, Mr. Thrale, then in a very unsatisfactory state of health, had been falsely denounced as a papist; and as there were also rioters at Bath, Mrs. Thrale and Fanny decided that it would be best to quit that place, and travel about the country. They started for Brighton; but before they got to Salisbury, London was again, in Dr. Burney's words, "the most secure residence in the kingdom." For the remainder of the year 1780, Fanny seems to have stayed quietly at St. Martin's Street and Chessington. In March, 1781, she came to town to find the Thrales settled for the time in a hired house in Grosvenor Square and talking vaguely of continental travel — to Spa, to Italy, and elsewhere. But Mr. Thrale was obviously growing worse; and in April he died suddenly of apoplexy, "on the morning of a day on which half the fashion of London had been invited to an intended assembly at his house." His death threw an infinity of additional care upon his already over-burdened widow; but, as soon as she was able, she again summoned Miss Burney to Streatham Place, where, off and on, she lived until September. Then "Daddy" Crisp, descending from his Surrey retreat, bore her away perforce to Chessington; and at Chessington she continued to stay until the beginning of 1782, when she returned to Newton House in order to be present at her sister Susan's marriage at St. Martin's Church to Captain Molesworth Phillips of the Marines, a comrade, in Cook's last voyage, of James Burney. After this, Fanny remained for some time quietly at home.

The reason why Dr. Burney wished to get his daughter away from Streatham Place, and why, at last, Mr. Crisp fetched her thence, — may perhaps be guessed. She had begun to work upon another novel; and her long absences from home seriously interfered with its progress. During the latter half of 1780, she had written steadily; but, in the following year, her renewed intercourse with Mrs. Thrale once more interrupted her labours; and her two fathers grew anxious that she should lose no further time. Of the advantages up to a certain point of her connection with the Streatham circle, both of them had been fully aware — Crisp especially. " Your time," he had written to her in April, 1780, " could not be better employed, for all your St. Martin's daddy wanted to retain you for some other purpose. You are now at school, the great school of the world, where swarms of new ideas and new characters will continually present themselves before you, —

> ' which you 'll draw in,
> As we do air, fast as 'tis ministered.' " [1]

But there must be a limit, even to schooling; and that limit, in the opinion of Dr. Burney and his friend, had now been reached. So Fanny saw no more of Streatham or Mrs. Thrale till her new book was finished.

[1] *Cymbeline*, Act I. Sc. i.

CHAPTER V

CECILIA — AND AFTER

EITHER from Mr. Crisp's injunctions as to secrecy, or
from suppressions in the *Diary* as we now have it, Miss
Burney's record contains but few references to the
progress of *Cecilia* — which was the name of the new
book. And these references occur chiefly in her letters
to her critic at Chessington. As already stated, there
had been a shadowy "Cecilia," with an imperilled
fortune, in the comedy of *The Witlings*. In December,
1779, Miss Burney had shown her "Daddy" a sketch
of a fresh heroine (then apparently called "Albina");
and he speaks of this fresh heroine's story in the
following April as a "new and striking" idea, affording, among other advantages, "a large field for
unhackneyed characters, observations, [and] subjects
for satire and ridicule." It further appears that the
Cecilia or Albina in question was to be "unbeautiful"
but "clever," — a deviation from the conventional in
which (whether she carried it out or not) Miss Burney
must have anticipated some of her distinguished suc-
cessors. Ten months later, in February, 1781, she is
hard at work. "I think I shall always hate this book
which has kept me so long away from you, as much
as I shall always love *Evelina*, who first *comfortably*

introduced me to you," — she tells Mrs. Thrale. Then,
— a year later still, — after the long interruption in
her task following upon Mr. Thrale's death, there
are groanings over the labour of transcription, — a
volume (and there are five) takes a fortnight, — impatience on her father's part for publication, — the usual
nervous apprehensions of hopeless failure, and much
defence and discussion of detail with "Daddy" Crisp.
At last, — when Mrs. Thrale has declared that *Evelina*
was but a baby to the new venture; and the cautious
critic of Chessington, protesting that there had been
nothing like it since Fielding and Smollett, has rashly
proclaimed his willingness to ensure its rapid and
universal success for half-a-crown, — on Friday the 12th
July, 1782, *Cecilia; or, Memoirs of an Heiress: By the
Author of Evelina*, price 12s. 6d., sewed, is published by
Messrs. Payne and Cadell, in five *duodecimo* volumes.
The first edition was of two thousand copies; and the
price paid to the author for the copyright, £250.[1] As
the Payne above mentioned was none other than the
friend of the family, "Honest Tom Payne" of the
Mews' Gate, afterwards James Burney's father-in-law,
it may fairly be assumed that this amount, trifling as
it must seem, — contrasted with the sums received by
modern authors addressing larger audiences under
different conditions, — was not considered inadequate
by Fanny's advisers. Indeed, from a chance reference

[1] Charlotte Burney in *Early Diary*, 1889, ii. 307. Lord
Macaulay (*Edinburgh Review*, lxxvi. 540) had been told that the
publishers gave two thousand pounds. Probably — as Mrs. Ellis
does not fail to suggest — there was some confusion on the
part of Macaulay's informant between pounds paid and copies
printed.

in the *Memoirs* to the arrangement of "the Cecilian business," we may conclude that, upon this occasion, Dr. Burney himself took charge of the negotiations.

Neither for ingenuity nor novelty had the plot of Miss Burney's first story been remarkable. The plot of her second attempt, though still conventional, was somewhat more ambitious. Miss Cecilia Beverley, a young lady in her twenty-first year, is heir, not only to ten thousand pounds from her father, but to three thousand *per annum* from her uncle, the Dean of ——, to which latter inheritance is attached the restrictive condition that, should she marry, the happy man must take her name as well as her money. This turns out to be a very material detail in the novel. When the story begins, the Dean of —— is just dead; and Miss Beverley and her fortune, during the brief remainder of her minority, are left in the hands of three guardians — a fashionable and extravagant Mr. Harrel, a vulgar and miserly Mr. Briggs, and a very proud and pompous Mr. Delvile (of Delvile Castle). In the first chapter of the story, Cecilia is quitting Mrs. Charlton, with whom she has been staying, to take up her quarters in town with the Harrels, — Mrs. Harrel, in her green and salad days, having been the heroine's "most favourite young friend." In London, where would-be suitors — most of them attracted to the *beaux yeux de sa cassette* — cluster about her like flies round a honey pot, she speedily becomes aware that the play-mate of her youth is terribly "translated" by the dissipations of a London life, that her friend's husband is an irredeemable gamester, and that both are palpably on the down-grade. Her available means become speedily involved in Harrel's ever-urgent necessities;

and the crisis of this part of the narrative is reached, about the middle of volume three, by his suicide in a very melodramatic fashion at Vauxhall Gardens, where, for the nonce, the chief personages in the book are ingeniously assembled. After Harrel's death, Cecilia goes to stay at Delvile Castle. Here an attachment already begun with the son, Mortimer Delvile, a young man at once excitable and irresolute, is further developed. But now the dead hand comes in. The haughty Delviles cannot bring themselves to consent to the change of the family name, even "for a consideration" of £3000 per annum. There are consequently scenes, in one of which Mrs. Delvile, after using extremely exaggerated expressions, exclaims "My brain is on fire!"—and breaks a blood vessel. Eventually, after she has been softened by illness, a suggestion is made that Cecilia shall surrender her uncle's fortune, with its vexatious obligations, and content herself with her Mortimer and her patrimony of ten thousand pounds. Unfortunately for this proposition, the ten thousand pounds in question are now non-existent, having been absorbed by the creditors of Harrel and others,—that is to say, by the Jews. After this, a private marriage takes place, with the connivance of Mrs. Delvile. But Cecilia's troubles are not yet at an end. Fresh and very unforeseen complications arise, and, for a brief period, she goes as mad as Clementina or Clarissa. At length the curtain comes down upon a Johnsonian passage in which she is left exhibiting the pensive and reluctant optimism of *Rasselas*.

If, in the foregoing rapid summary, it has not always been possible to speak with uniform gravity, it is that,

to-day, the main issue of Cecilia's story has become —
as the author's own Captain Aresby would now have
said — a little *démodé*. In the present year of grace, it
is difficult to comprehend the social conditions which
should prevent a sensible man from marrying the
woman he loves (particularly if that woman have
£3000 a year) simply because the concomitant surrender of his family name would — as Mrs. Delvile
puts it — bring "the blood of his wronged ancestors
into his guilty cheeks." But when *Cecilia* was written,
this was an other-guess matter; and the point was not
only seriously argued by bishops, peers and ladies of
quality, but was thought by no means undeserving of
anxious consideration. A noble Lord, who descended
from Elfrida, and had a castle in Warwickshire, was
distinctly of opinion that the obstructive attitude of
Mr. Delvile *père* was a correct one; while Mrs. Thrale,
who dated from Adam of Salzburg — one of the companions of the Conqueror — was equally convinced that
her mother, Mrs. Salusbury, would have done just what
Mrs. Delvile did. But this debatable point apart,
Cecilia's story is unquestionably clever. The characters
— and there are a crowd of them — are clearly drawn
and discriminated; the pictures of contemporary social
life are varied and very lively, while the famous Vauxhall episode, if it be not precisely the tragic masterpiece which it seemed to the fond eyes of admiring
"Daddy" Crisp, certainly contrives to hold the reader
in a genuine suspense of curiosity until the final event
is reached. The discussion between the mother and
son, — the other "crack scene" of the book — that,
indeed, for which the author declares she wrote the
whole, Mr. Crisp did not approve so much, and he

was right. If it did not impress him, it impresses us
still less. Mrs. Delvile's stormy heroics seem out of
all proportion to the gravity of the matter in hand,
and an unsympathetic reader, bewildered by the hail
of commination, may well be forgiven for wondering
whether the cause is worthy of the clamour. Nevertheless Miss Burney, in clinging to her convictions
in regard to "name-compelling" wills, as well as in declining to end her book "like the hack Italian operas,
with a jolly chorus that makes all parties good and all
parties happy," was only acting in strict accordance
with the injunctions, received from more than one
adviser, to rely upon her own instincts, and not to
depart from them, when her mind was made up. And
it is a feature of her character, that, notwithstanding
her undoubted distrust of her powers, she was sometimes as restive and intractable under criticism as
Richardson himself.

The two scenes above indicated are those which are
most frequently referred to by Miss Burney's critics.
But there are others which, if not as highly-wrought,
are as worthy of praise. The opera rehearsal, — at
which it was said the book always opened, — the
description of the *ton* parties, the long masquerade
chapter, and the dialogue between Albany, Briggs and
Hobson on Charity (which may be compared with that
on the same subject between Parson Adams and
Mr. Peter Pounce in *Joseph Andrews*), are well worth
reading. But the names remind us that Miss Burney
is, primarily, what Johnson called her, a "character-
monger," and that her plot is subordinate to her personages. Some of these, in spite of her protests, she
had evidently seen in the flesh; some she had half-seen

or overheard; some she had wholly invented from current social characteristics.   Mr. Meadows, the absent-
minded and affectedly-indifferent, and Captain Aresby,
who interlards his conversation with French words
like the coming Silver Fork School and the lady in
Thackeray's *Almack's Adieu* — are probably examples
from the last category.   Mr. Monckton and the supercilious Sir Robert Floyer, the caustic Mr. Gosport
and the voluble Miss Larolles, she had doubtless met;
while in those days of gaming and E.O. tables, she had
probably heard of many Mr. Harrels.   As to the miserly
and penurious Briggs (and the facility with which one
can label Miss Burney's characters with defining ad-
jectives indicates one of her limitations), the consensus
of contemporary criticism seems to have decided that
he was overdrawn.   But he is certainly not more
exaggerated than some of the later characters of Dickens, and he is distinctly amusing, especially in his
encounters with "Don Pedigree," as he calls his colleague, Mr. Delvile.   Hobson the builder, with his
large and puffy presence, his red waistcoat, and his
round curled wig, is a capital specimen of the bumptious
prosperous tradesman; while the thin, mean-looking,
cringing and obsequious Mr. Simkins (the hosier) is
another excellently observed and contrasted variety.
Morrice, the pushing and officious young lawyer, the
versatile Belfield, and that vivacious "agreeable Rattle"
of rank, Lady Honoria Pemberton, can only be named.
Lastly — for we must omit others altogether — comes
Johnson's favourite Albany, — a cross between Ape-
mantus and Solomon Eagle, — whose stagy denuncia-
tions certainly warrant the ingenuous inquiry of Mr.
Hobson whether "the gentleman might be speaking

something by heart." There should be an original for
Albany; but he has not been definitely revealed.

Cecilia is more elaborate and much more mature
than *Evelina*. It is also more skilfully constructed,
and more carefully, though not so naturally, written.
But it is certainly too long; and towards the close
suggests something of the hurry imposed upon the
author by her eager father. It must also be confessed
that the last chapters are scarcely as interesting as
their forerunners. As to the success of the book
with its first audience, however, there can be no
doubt. Anxiously awaited, it was welcomed with the
warmest enthusiasm by numbers of readers; and by
no one more splendidly and royally than by Edmund
Burke, whose acquaintance Fanny had made at Sir
Joshua's not very long before it appeared. When
it came out, Burke wrote her a long letter, which
was reprinted with subsequent editions. Few (he
told her), let their experience in life and manners
be what it might, would not find themselves better
informed concerning human nature, and their stock
of observation enriched, by reading *Cecilia*. " You
have," he went on, " crowded into a few small volumes
an incredible variety of characters; most of them well
planned, well supported, and well contrasted with each
other. If there be any fault in this respect, it is one
in which you are in no great danger of being imitated.
Justly as your characters are drawn, perhaps they are
too numerous. But I beg pardon; I fear it is quite
in vain to preach economy to those who are come
young to excessive and sudden opulence." Praising
her humour, her pathos, her " comprehensive and noble
moral," and her sagacious observations, he concluded, —

"In an age distinguished by producing extraordinary women, I hardly dare to tell you where my opinion would place you amongst them. I respect your modesty, that will not endure the commendations which your merit forces from everybody." A few months later, she met Burke at the house of the Hon. Miss Monckton (the "Lydia White" of that age), when he was equally kind, though he ventured upon some criticisms. He thought the masquerade scene too long, and that something might be spared from Harrel's grand assembly; he did not like Morrice's part at the Pantheon;[1] and he wished the conclusion "either more happy or more miserable." With this last Fanny — as we have already seen — could not coincide; but he promptly consoled her by another compliment. Nothing had struck him so much as the admirable skill with which her ingenious characters made themselves known by their own words; and he congratulated her upon her conquest of some of the old wits, because of the difficulty of giving satisfaction to those who piqued themselves on being past receiving it. Also, he touched upon the amount she had obtained from Payne and Cadell for the copyright, which he evidently knew. "Why did you not send for your own friend out of the city [*i.e.* Mr. Briggs]? He would have taken care you should not part with it [*Cecilia*] so much below par."

Her older admirers were as kind. Sir Joshua was perpetually bringing her intelligence of something which had been said to her advantage; and Johnson came no whit behind. Instructing Susy Thrale, who had just put up her hair, and assumed womanly garb,

---

[1] Book iv. ch. 2.

he directed her, with mock solemnity, how to "increase
her consequence" by censuring *Cecilia* — much in the
manner in which the author of the *Female Quixote*
had recommended his own *Rambler:* "Tell the world
how ill it was conceived, and how ill executed. Tell
them how little there is in it of human nature, and
how well your knowledge of the world enables you
to judge of the failings in that book. Find fault
without fear; and if you are at a loss for any to find,
invent whatever comes into your mind, for you may
say what you please, with little fear of detection, since
of those who praise *Cecilia* not half have read it, and
of those who have read it, not half remember it. Go
to work, therefore, boldly; and particularly mark that
the character of Albany is extremely unnatural, to
your own knowledge, since you never met with such
a man at Mrs. Cummyn's School." A year later, his
enthusiasm was still unabated. "Sir"—he said to
Boswell—"if you talk of *Cecilia*, talk on." From
other sources came commendations as pleasant. Mrs.
Chapone, who, as Miss Mulso, had cried over *Clarissa*,
could not, for very excess of eagerness, cry at all over
Cecilia. "I was in an agitation that half killed me,
that shook all my nerves," — she told the author, —
"and made me unable to sleep at nights from the suspense I was in." Mrs. Walsingham, the witty daughter
of the wit Sir Charles Hanbury Williams, related how
Queen Charlotte herself had spoken of the book, and
criticised Mr. Briggs; while, from another source,
came tidings that Gibbon had read it in a day, which
was a third of the time that even Burke had taken.
But Miss Burney's supreme and full dress laureation
came at Mrs. Ord's in Queen Anne's Street from that

ancient *bel esprit* and conversationist, Soame Jenyns, then nearing eighty, who, arriving by arrangement, attired in a Court suit of apricot-coloured silk lined with white satin, regaled the author of *Cecilia* with a magnificent and magniloquent harangue upon the merits of her work, to which the rest of the distinguished company respectfully listened — standing!

But if *Cecilia* pleased the old wit, Soame Jenyns, it did not equally please the old wit, Horace Walpole, to whom it suggested many of the inconvenient objections of the incorruptible. He thought it "immeasurably long"; he disliked the end (as Burke did); he found most of the personages *outrés ;* he said (and, in this instance, unanswerably) that they spoke too uniformly in character to be true to the complexity of human life; and he wished Albany suppressed altogether. The book, also, he complained, "was written in Dr. Johnson's unnatural phrase." Other people — either in praise or blame — had made the same discovery. "The particularly nervous and perspicuous style" — wrote the *Monthly Review*—" appears to have been framed on the best model of Dr. Johnson." But even among Fanny's friends, there were those to whom this was scarcely a merit. "The writing here and there" — wrote Mr. Twining of Colchester to Fanny's father — "is not the better for a little imitation (probably involuntary) of Dr. Johnson." That there are traces of the Johnsonian manner in *Evelina* has already been observed, especially where Miss Burney writes in her own person. In *Cecilia* these evidences would naturally be more manifest, since the narrative form is substituted for the epistolary. Still there is little

of the Doctor in the many conversations, and the point
may easily be overlaboured. There is enough, however, to warrant Boswell in claiming Miss Burney as
one of Johnson's many imitators; and Lord Macaulay
picked out one passage in special which has the very
trick and turn of the great man's pen. But when it
led Lord Macaulay to say, as he did, that he had not
the smallest doubt that Johnson had " revised" *Cecilia*,
and " retouched the style of many passages," he was
demonstrably in error. " I never saw one word of it
before it was printed,"—the Doctor told a gentleman
who wished "to make out some credit to him from the
little rogue's book"; and the disclaimer must surely
be accepted as decisive.[1]   At the same time, Johnson
was undoubtedly the reigning model; and, consciously
or unconsciously, Miss Burney copied him. " Fanny
carries bird-lime in her brains "—said her father—
" for everything that lights there sticks." As the writer
of *Evelina*, she had remembered the writer of the
Rambler; and nothing is more reasonable than that
she should remember him all the more in *Cecilia*, when,
by personal contact and personal admiration, she had
absorbed and assimilated his method and vocabulary.
Whether she would not have done better to copy herself, is another matter.

In July, 1782, when *Cecilia* was published, Fanny
Burney was thirty,—that critical age before which,
according to a discouraging dictum, those who are not
doomed to failure, must have contrived to succeed.
Hitherto, she *had* succeeded; and if a bard in the
Morning Herald was to be believed, had now taken

---

[1] *Diary and Letters*, 1892, i. 454.

her place permanently in that galaxy of which Burke
had written, for

"Little Burney's quick discerning "

was duly bracketed with

" Carter's piety and learning," —

with the " pathetic pen " of Hannah More, the " pointed
wit " of Mrs. Cowley (of *The Belle's Stratagem*), with

" Smiling Streatfield's ivory neck,
Nose and notions — *à la Grecque*,"

and all the varied virtues of Mrs. Chapone, Mrs.
Boscawen, Mrs. Thrale, and Mrs. Montagu.[1]   Her
friends were naturally anxious that she should pursue
her triumphs; and " Daddy " Crisp, while piously
enjoining her not " to remit her ardour and industry to
be perfect," and sagaciously observing " that there had
been more instances than one, where writers have wrote
themselves down, by slovenliness, laziness, and pre-
suming too much on public favour for what is past," —
was still very practically alive to the necessities of
taking the tide at the flood.   " This is the harvest time
of your life," — he wrote; " your sun shines hot; lose
not a moment, then, but make your hay directly.
'Touch the yellow boys,' — as Briggs says — 'grow
warm '; make the booksellers come down handsomely
— count the ready — the chink."   Nevertheless, it was
fourteen years before Miss Burney published another
novel; and we must now revert to the chronicle of her
life.

[1] The verses from which these quotations are taken appeared in
the *Morning Herald* for 12 March, 1782. Long attributed to Sir
W. W. Pepys, they are now given to Dr. Burney. But, as regards
his daughter, they only express a general feeling.

K

There can be little doubt that the publication of *Cecilia* largely extended the circle of her acquaintance; and that the paternal coach must often have been in requisition to convey her to the houses of the "lyon-hunters." "I begin to grow most heartily sick and fatigued"— she writes in December, 1782 — "of this continual round of visiting, and these eternal new acquaintances." Elsewhere there are indications that, for one who was not able to run milliners' bills, the question of costume must have been an absorbing one. "Miss Burney"—said Mr. Cambridge—"had no time to write, for she was always working at her clothes." Mr. Richard Owen Cambridge of Twickenham, — Walpole's "Cambridge the Everything,"—now an elderly gentleman, was one of the new friends who seem to have specially attracted her; and there is an account in the *Diary* of a visit she made in the summer of 1783 to that pleasant house of his in the meadows by Richmond Bridge, to which so many old-world notabilities were wont to resort. One of the things she recalls is her host's testimony — in spite of the *Préjugé à la mode* — to his love for his wife. "There is no sight so pleasing to me," he told her, "as seeing Mrs. Cambridge enter a room; and that after having been married to her for forty years." At Mrs. Vesey's she met Cambridge's near neighbour, Horace Walpole, whom she found extremely entertaining. Dr. Parr, Jonas Hanway, *Tasso* Hoole, Benjamin West, the Wartons, Mrs. Ord, Mrs. Buller, Mrs. Chapone, Mrs. Garrick, also flit through her pages, though it would be impossible to make record of them here. But among the "fair females"—as "the General" of the last chapter would have said — may be mentioned, chiefly

because she must be mentioned hereafter, Mme. de
Genlis, then in this country. To this most fascinating
and insidious personage, Miss Burney was at first much
attracted. But the acquaintance — her niece and editor
tells us — was not maintained; and Fanny afterwards
made nearer and dearer French friends for whom the
multifarious author of *Adèle et Théodore* was only
"*cette coquine de Brulard.*"

Upon the dissolution of the Whig Ministry at the
close of 1783, Burke, as Paymaster General, appointed
Dr. Burney organist of Chelsea Hospital Chapel, at an
increased salary of £50 per annum. It was not much,
but it was enhanced by the courteous way in which it
was done. In her father's absence, Burke himself
informed Miss Burney of what he styled his "last act
in office." Earlier — in the same year, 1783 — had come
her first serious bereavement since she had lost her
mother, — the death of her kind old Mentor at Chessington. By this time, Mr. Crisp was seventy-six, and had
long been a martyr to the gout to which he finally
succumbed. During his last illness, Fanny wrote to
him frequently and affectionately; and, when it grew
grave, hastened to his bed-side. She was "the dearest
thing to him on earth," he told her with his last breath;
and her sorrow at his loss was for the time overwhelm-
ing. In what was once the picturesque and rustic, but
is now the "restored" and "enlarged" church at Chessington, is a mural tablet to his memory, with an
epitaph in verse by Dr. Burney, which his daughter
has printed.[1] To Fanny the loss of "Daddy" Crisp
was incalculable, for he had been at once her most
judicious admirer and her most stimulating critic, never

[1] *Memoirs of Dr. Burney*, 1832, ii. 323.

failing to mingle blame with his praise — blame against
which, after the manner of the criticised, she generally
at first protested. He was a better counsellor than her
father, who was too eager for publication to be always
mindful of the necessity for finish. Yet, at the same
time, Crisp was urgent that his favourite should trust
her own instincts. " Who[m]soever you think fit to consult, let their talents and tastes be ever so great, hear
what they say, allowed ! — agreed !— but never give up
or alter a tittle merely on their authority, nor unless it
perfectly coincides with your own inward feelings. I
can say this to my sorrow and to my cost. But mum ! "
Which last injunction was no doubt a reference to his
own ill-starred *Virginia*.

More than a year later took place what may almost
be regarded as another bereavement, — the second
marriage of Mrs. Thrale. With this much-discussed
event, — perplexed, moreover, by no little pique and
wounded feeling, — we are concerned only in so far
as it relates to Miss Burney. Gabriele Piozzi, who is
sometimes contemptuously and erroneously described
as a merely obscure " fiddler," was a musician and professional singer of exceptional ability, who, according
to contemporary prints, was earning some £1200 per
annum by his talents. He was a Roman Catholic, a
handsome man " with gentle, pleasing, unaffected
manners," of unimpeachable integrity, and about six
months older than Mrs. Thrale, who, at her husband's
death, was forty. The Thrales first made his acquaintance at Brighton in 1780, and he speedily became a
" prodigious favourite." After her husband's death,
Mrs. Thrale's liking for him gradually increased until it
became a passion. Meanwhile, in 1782, with Johnson's

full concurrence, Streatham Place was let for three years to Lord Shelburne; and after leaving it in October of that year, the Doctor went with her for six weeks to her Brighton house — a fact which takes off something from the pathetic poignancy of the famous *adieux* to Streatham, regretful and melancholy as they must of necessity have been. Before 1782 had closed Mrs. Thrale had determined to marry Piozzi. But her daughters — to whom their father had left £20,000 each — were against the match; and after much mental perplexity, she decided to bid her lover farewell, and did so in January 1783. The sacrifice, however, proved beyond her powers; her health began to suffer; and a year later, with the tacit consent of her children, Piozzi was recalled from Milan, and she was married to him on the 23rd July, 1784, according to the rites of the Romish Church, by the Chaplain of the Spanish Ambassador. A second marriage followed on the 25th at St. James's Church, Bath. Her correspondence with Johnson, upon what he regarded as this "ignominious" union, has been printed by Mr. Hayward, and *her* letters should be read as well as those of the Doctor.[1]

In all these proceedings, between Fanny's affection for Mrs. Thrale and her affection for Dr. Johnson, she played a delicate and a difficult part. According to Mrs. Thrale, it was Fanny who had first introduced Piozzi to her as " a man likely to lighten the burden of life to her." In October, 1782, Mrs. Thrale writes in *Thraliana* that that " dear little discerning creature, Fanny Burney," says she is in love with Piozzi; and she then goes on to argue the *pros* and *cons* with herself.

---

[1] *Autobiography, etc., of Mrs. Piozzi* (*Thrale*), 1861 (2nd ed.), i. 147 *et seq.*

At Brighton, just before the first farewell to Piozzi, Mrs. Thrale admits that Fanny's "interest as well as judgment goes all against my marriage"—a view which is fully confirmed by Miss Burney's absolute refusal to approve the course proposed, although at the same time she found it difficult to restrain her indignation at Queenie's heartless attitude to her mother. Later still, she said decidedly that Mrs. Thrale must either marry Piozzi instantly or give him up, otherwise her reputation would be lost. In May, 1784, Mrs. Thrale having decided to marry Piozzi, came to London to consult Miss Burney about details. The meeting, as may be divined, was embarrassing to Fanny, who, in Mrs. Thrale's words, was as much "pained as delighted by her visit." Nevertheless she gave her time wholly to her old friend, and her father was also consulted. Dr. Burney, a brother professional himself, regarded the matter more philosophically than some of his nicely sensitive contemporaries. "No one"—he said—"could blame Piozzi for accepting a gay young widow. What could he do better?" Then came the marriage, with a sequel which might have been foreseen. Mrs. Thrale considered that Fanny's congratulations upon a step "which she had uniformly, openly, and with deep and avowed affliction, thought wrong"—were insufficiently cordial. The *Diary* only contains a sketch of Miss Burney's answer to this impeachment—an answer by which Mrs. Piozzi, preoccupied with her own happiness, could scarcely be gravely disturbed. She besought her "sweetest Burney" to give herself no serious concern in the matter, to "quiet her kind heart," and to love Mr. Piozzi, if she loved his wife. To this "F. B." sent "the warmest and most heartfelt"

rejoinder.   And there the six years' correspondence
ended.   Miss Burney may have been right in connecting its cessation with resentment on Piozzi's part,
"when he was informed of her constant opposition
to the union," but there were surely reasons enough
in the circumstances of the case to make further intercourse difficult, if not impracticable.

A heavier loss, however, than that of Mrs. Thrale,
was in store for Fanny Burney.   Johnson, who was
now seventy-four, had for some time been perceptibly
failing.   In the middle of 1783 he had a stroke; and
at the end of the same year, he had been very ill with
spasmodic asthma.   "Ah! *priez Dieu pour moi!*" — he
had said suddenly to her, as she sat by him; and he
had been "quite touchingly affectionate."   She was his
"dearest of all dear ladies," — he declared.   A year
later he was manifestly nearing his end; and on
Thursday, the 25th November, 1784, Fanny saw him
for the last time.   Though exceedingly ill, he received
her; and they had a long conversation in the old way,
— about his dead wife — about Queenie Thrale, who had
been to visit him, — about Queenie's mother, from whom
he never hears, and to whom he never writes.   "I
drive her," he said, "quite from my mind.   If I meet
with one of her letters, I burn it instantly.   I have
burnt all I can find.   I never speak of her, and I desire
never to hear of her more.   I drive her, as I said,
wholly from my mind."[1]   Fanny quickly changed the

---

[1] This was the bitterness of the sick bed; and it is wholly
irreconcilable with the regard expressed in Johnson's last communication to Mrs. Piozzi and his gratitude "for that kindness
which soothed twenty years of a life radically wretched."
Luckily for her, he did not burn *all* her letters, for her not
undignified answer to his first rough remonstrance was found

subject; and he went on to talk of the "Bristol milk-
woman," Ann Yearsley, a local poetess whom Hannah
More befriended, — of Shakespeare and his Caliban,
and other topics. At length, seeing he grew visibly
worse, she rose to go ; and, for the first time she could
remember, he did not oppose it. But kindly pressing
both her hands, he begged her to come again — to come
soon, and to remember him in her prayers. She never
saw him afterwards, although she more than once
essayed to do so. When, two days before his death,
Dr. Burney called, the old man spoke of her tenderly,
reiterated his request about her prayers; and then,
brightening for a moment, said, almost archly, "I think
I shall throw the ball at Fanny yet!" Apparently
also, he asked to see her. But although, on the following morning, she waited tearfully in the cold little
parlour at Bolt Court, and lingered on the stairs that led
to the back room where he lay, no summons came from
the sick man. At length arrived Bennet Langton with a
faltering message. The Doctor hoped she would excuse
him ; but he felt himself too weak for such an interview.

With Johnson dead, and Crisp dead, and Mrs. Piozzi
alienated by her marriage, life — it may be imagined —
must, in these days, have seemed unusually gloomy to
Fanny Burney. But fortunately, though her feelings
were strong, her temperament was elastic. And the
successful author of *Cecilia* had now troops of friends,
both new and old. To those she respected, it was her
nature to grow rapidly and devotedly attached. Even
for some weeks before Johnson's fatal illness, her

by Miss Hawkins amongst his papers, and returned to its
writer. As already stated, it is printed by Hayward (*Autobiography*, etc., 1861 (2nd ed.), i. 240–1, No. 4).

letters had been dated from Norbury — a charming
country-house upon a hill-slope in Surrey, looking
southward across the Mole and the beautiful Vale of
Mickleham, to Dorking and Box Hill.   Here — in addition to a park with a Druids' Grove of yews that dated
from Domesday Book, and a saloon with trellised
ceiling, where the landscapes of George Barret cun-
ningly completed the magnificent view from the
windows — she enjoyed the companionship of a host
and hostess, who, if not as remarkable as her Streatham friends, were at least as cultured and as kind.
Mr. Locke of Norbury was a genuine connoisseur,
who had brought the Discobolus of Myron to England,
while his son William, a youth of seventeen, was to
become a capable historical artist.   Mrs. Locke, — the
"dearest Fredy " of the *Diary,* according to Miss Burney,
was " sweet and most bewitching."   At Norbury, where,
on fine days, they wandered in the grounds; or on wet
days, read Mme. de Sévigné and Captain Cook aloud in
the picture room, Fanny seems to have been thoroughly
content to " stay till she *must* go," driving unpleasant
thought away like "a wasp near an open window."
What was more, she was in a sense *en pays de connais-
sance,* for Norbury was only six miles from that other
regretted " place of peace, ease, freedom and cheerfulness," Chessington Hall.   During the next few months
her visits to the Lockes were frequent; and in later
years, she was to know them even better still.   Meanwhile, to her delight, her sister Susan made Mickleham
her residence, occupying with her husband and family
a little cottage on the high road at the very foot of
Norbury Park.

But besides her relations with the Lockes of Norbury,

she formed, at this date, another friendship, of which
the consequences, during the years that immediately
followed, were of no small importance. Early in 1783,
she had been taken by Mrs. Chapone to visit the
venerable Mrs. Delany (the widow of Swift's friend,
Dr. Patrick Delany), then living in London at St.
James's Place. At this time, Mrs. Delany was eighty-
three, a charming and accomplished old lady, with a
reputation for cutting out the ingenious "paper
Mosaiks" now in the British Museum ; a great favourite with King George and Queen Charlotte; and the
bosom friend of another old lady and *grande dame*,
Prior's "Peggy," the Dowager Duchess of Portland.
Both Mrs. Delany and her friend (who arrived shortly
after Fanny reached St. James's Place) had been prejudiced against *Cecilia*, — the Duchess chiefly from recollections of the cruel depression into which she had
been thrown by the tedium and the tragedy of Richardson's *Clarissa*. But they had both succumbed to
Fanny's book ; they knew its characters by heart ;
told stories how lords and prelates had discussed the
incidents and the characters, and finally crowned their
commendations by praising its excellent tone and
morality. "No book" — said Mrs. Delany — "ever was
so useful as this, because none other that is so good
was ever so much read." And the Duchess and Mrs.
Chapone said *ditto* to Mrs. Delany. Mrs. Chapone, by
the way, told an interesting anecdote. Someone, she
said, had been protesting that there could be no such
character as Briggs, whom not only Queen Charlotte but
Mrs. Thrale had regarded as exaggerated.[1] Thereupon

[1] Other people think so still. Mr. Bryce (*Studies in Contemporary Biography*, 1903, i. 127) speaks of Briggs and Miss

" a poor, little mean city man" in company had "started up, and said—' But there is though, for I'se one myself.'"

The friendship thus inaugurated speedily became enduring; and Fanny's record for 1784 contains more than one reference to days spent at St. James's Place, sometimes *en tête-à-tête*, when she was allowed to rummage Mrs. Delany's correspondence with Swift and Young or listen to her old stories of the notabilities of the first half of the century. In July, 1785, the Duchess of Portland died; and the loss drew Fanny closer to her new friend. Another result of the Duchess's death was, that it deprived Mrs. Delany of the summer quarters which she had for so many years enjoyed at Bulstrode, the seat of the Portlands near Beaconsfield. Upon learning this, the King and Queen, whose affection for Mrs. Delany seems to have been of the most genuine kind, offered her a small house near the gate of Windsor Castle, which, with the greatest forethought, they immediately stocked and put in order for her, the King himself personally superintending the workmen. They also gave her a pension of £300 a year, which, in order that it might escape taxation, the good-natured Queen herself was accustomed to hand to her half-yearly in a pocket-book. Pending Mrs. Delany's removal to Windsor, Fanny was

---

Larolles as " so exaggerated, as to approach the grotesque." Nevertheless, as is often the case, Briggs has been more satisfactorily identified with a living model than any other of Miss Burney's characters. In Mrs. Ellis's "Preface" and Notes to *Cecilia*, she shows conclusively that, designedly or undesignedly, Briggs reproduces many of the traits of a personage already mentioned in these pages, Nollekens the sculptor. (See *ante*, p. 51, and J. T. Smith's *Nollekens and his Times*, 2 vols. 1828.)

often in attendance on her, either as companion or
sympathiser. When, at last, she departed, Fanny
went to Norbury, and elsewhere. But in November,
1785, she was again "domesticated" with Mrs. Delany
at Windsor.

One of the first things which she heard upon her
arrival was, that Their Majesties had been expecting
her. All the Princesses were coming to see her — she
was told. Moreover, the Queen, stimulated by Mme.
de Genlis' praises of Miss Burney, had been re-reading
Cecilia, or rather having it read to her by one of her
readers, the Swiss geologist, M. de Luc. (As M. de
Luc could hardly speak four words of English, this
must have been unfortunate for *Cecilia*.) The book
had also been read to the Princess Elizabeth. These
announcements, and the particular inquiries which
the King and Queen did not cease to make about
her of Mrs. Delany, naturally filled Fanny with all her
customary trepidations, real and imaginary. Owing,
however, to the illness of the Princess Elizabeth and
other causes, the meeting did not at once take place.
Then suddenly, on Friday, December 16, "a large
man, in deep mourning," and with a star glittering on
his breast, made sudden apparition in Mrs. Delany's
drawing room, throwing its occupants into petrified
confusion. It was King George himself. He spoke
very kindly to Miss Burney, showing much benevolent
consideration for her nervousness; but overwhelmed
her presently by questions after the "What! What!"
fashion, made familiar by the *Probationary Odes* and
the irreverent performances of " Peter Pindar." How
did she write *Evelina* — and why ? Why did she not
tell her father ? How was it printed ? Why had she

done nothing more since *Cecilia?* To which last
Fanny answered demurely and hesitatingly that she
believed she had exhausted herself — a reply which
was received in the light of a *bon mot*. During the
progress of this inquisition, which is recorded with
extreme minuteness, arrived Queen Charlotte, to whom
His Majesty forthwith carefully recapitulated his conversation with Miss Burney. The Queen, who was very
soft-voiced and gracious, was equally curious. She
wished much to know if there was to be "nothing
more"; and she was good enough to express a desire
that there should be something. From what had been
done, she thought there was a power to do good. And
good to young people was so very good a thing, that
she could not help wishing it could be. Thereupon the
King — as one behind the scenes — proceeded to assure
her that Miss Burney had made no vow not to write;
— it was only a question of inclination — was it not?
They were, both of them, evidently prepossessed in
favour of Mrs. Delany's young friend, who, on her side,
does ample justice to the unaffected, gentle dignity
of Queen Charlotte; the *bonhomie*, good spirits, and
friendly kindness of the King; and the fondness of
the royal couple for one another.

A few days later, the King came again to tea,
chatting very freely in his discursive way of many
things, — of Mme. de Genlis' knowledge of English;
of the "monster" Voltaire; of the pride and ingrati-
tude of Rousseau (to whom His Majesty had given a
pension). But here Miss Burney was able to acquaint
him, on her father's authority, that M. Jean-Jacques
kept His Majesty's portrait over his chimney at Paris.
Then the King passed to the recent death of Kitty

Clive;[1] and the merits of Mrs. Siddons, whom he ranked above Garrick — an opinion from which Fanny could of course only mutely dissent. Shakespeare came next; and His Majesty — as is known — had the courage of his opinions. "Was there ever such stuff as great part of Shakespeare? only one must not say so! — But what think you? — What? — Is there not sad stuff? — What? — What?" And he instanced several plays and characters in support of his heresies. Fanny told him how Mme. de Genlis had declared that no woman ought to go to any of the English comedies, — an aspersion of the national stage which was resented with much animation by the discerning critic who had twice ordered the representation of *She Stoops to Conquer*. In a further "private conference" with his consort, there was more talk of Mme. de Genlis, who, it seems, always sent her "moral page" to Queen Charlotte; — of the *Sorrows of Werther*, which neither she nor Fanny admired as the great Napoleon did; — of an unnamed but meritorious work picked up for her upon a stall by one of her servants. "It is amazing what good books there are on stalls" — said the Queen — an utterance which should canonise her for ever with the book-hunter. She afterwards spoke of Klopstock's *Messiah*, criticising the author's engraftments upon the sacred story; and then gave an account of the Protestant nunneries in Germany, to one of which she had belonged, — of the rigid rules of entrance, — of the internal economy, — of the costume. The record of the interview breaks off abruptly; but it leaves a pleasant impression of Queen Charlotte's amenity, humour, and conversational powers.

[1] 6th December, 1785.

This meeting took place on December 20th, 1785, after which Miss Burney went home. She paid another visit to Windsor in the May following with her father, who was anxious to obtain the then vacant post of Master of the King's Band. To this end he was recommended to show himself to the King, when he walked upon the Terrace at Windsor; but not to make direct solicitation. Unhappily, the place had already been promised by the Lord Chamberlain; and though both the King and Queen spoke amiably to Miss Burney, the expedition was without effect. Very shortly afterwards, by the resignation of Mrs. Haggerdorn, Second Keeper of Robes, a vacancy occurred in the Royal Household. Mrs. Haggerdorn's place was much sought after, even by persons of fashion and rank. But the Queen had taken a fancy to Mrs. Delany's visitor, and offered it to Miss Burney. By Fanny herself the proposition was received with consternation. The separation from her family circle, the close confinement to the Court, the permanent character of an engagement so made, the wearisome "life of attendance and dependence" — we are using her own words — all these things she considered were unsuited to her inclinations, and unfavourable to her happiness. But her friends — who, it is only fair to remember, knew her literary limitations, and were better instructed as to her literary gains than some of her earlier critics — took a different view of the matter. The Lockes and her sister, Mrs. Phillips, had, indeed, always expected some such development of her Windsor visits; Mrs. Delany — a courtier in grain — was naturally transported; while her father (in whose hands she dutifully placed herself), and even Burke, regarded the royal offer as affording a certain prospect of an honourable and advantageous establishment for life. It was accordingly accepted, after an interview with the Queen, who, in the face of all the Windsor place-hunters, had made her own choice. "I was led to think of Miss Burney" — Her Majesty told Mrs. Delany — "first by her books; then by seeing her; then by always hearing how she was loved by her friends; but chiefly by your friendship for her." Of Fanny herself, Queen Charlotte asked no questions, only saying pleasantly — "I am sure we shall do very well together."

CHAPTER VI

THE QUEEN'S DRESSER

On the 6th of July, 1786, the *Public Advertiser* announced that — " Miss Burney, daughter of Dr. Burney, is appointed Dresser to the Queen, in the room of Mrs. Hoggadore, gone to Germany." The last three words were premature, for further notifications, with much pleasing and ingenious variation of Mrs. Haggerdorn's name, made it clear that the lady in question only took leave of the Queen on the 13th, and retired to her native Mecklenburg on the 17th. She is described in the public print aforesaid as Her Majesty's "confidential companion and dresser"; but in the Court Register she figures as one of two "Keepers of Robes," the Senior Keeper being a Mrs. Schwellenberg (or Schwellenbergen), who, with Mrs. Haggerdorn, had accompanied the Queen from Germany five and twenty years earlier. To Mrs. Haggerdorn's post, with some modification of duties, Miss Burney now succeeded, entering upon her office on the 17th July. As — for lack of repairs — Windsor Castle had been for some years uninhabitable, the Royal Family were at this time domiciled in two temporary buildings, described indifferently by topographers as "mansions" and "barracks." These had been built for the King by

Sir William Chambers. The larger, the Upper or
Queen's Lodge,[1] so called from its occupying the site
of a former Queen Anne's Lodge, was appropriated to
Queen Charlotte, King George and the two elder
Princesses — the Princess Royal and the Princess Augusta. It stood to the southeast of the Castle,
almost facing the South Terrace. Behind it was a
large walled garden, where Herschel exhibited newly
discovered comets to the Court; and at the end of
this garden was the second or Lower Lodge, allotted to
the younger branches of the Royal Family. Both
these structures were of stuccoed red brick, with
embattled copings. They were draughty and cold in
winter. Miss Burney's apartments, a bed-room and a
large drawing-room, were on the ground-floor in the
Upper Lodge. The drawing-room looked on the
Round Tower and the Terrace; and was probably at
the eastern corner, as she speaks of its opening at the
farther side, from the windows, to the Little Park,
which lay to the north and east of the Castle. The
bed-room (which was entered from the sitting-room)
looked into the garden. Immediately above her were
the rooms of her colleague, Mrs. Schwellenberg.
Fanny describes her quarters as "airy, pleasant, clean
and healthy," "delightfully independent of all the
rest of the house," and as containing "everything I can
desire for my convenience and comfort." Mrs. Delany

[1] There is a large oval print by James Fittler, after George
Robertson, dated 28th July, 1783, showing the Queen's Lodge
from the South Terrace, on which the Royal Party are taking
their evening promenade. In the background, to the left, at
the garden end, the Lower Lodge is to be distinguished. Both
Lodges were pulled down in 1823; and their site is now partly
occupied by the Royal Stables.

was not fifty yards away; and she could readily obtain access to the South Terrace by a special flight of steps, At Kew, to which Their Majesties frequently migrated, she had also her special accommodation, rather contracted, after the fashion of the place, but "tidy and comfortable enough"; and at St. James's Palace she occupied rooms, one of which looked over the Park. From other indications, it appears that she had her special man-servant; and, in common with Mrs. Schwellenberg, the use of a carriage. Her salary was £200 a year.

After a week, she began to realise her position and to draw up "a concise abstract of the general method of passing the day." Concise though it be, it is too detailed to be reproduced entire, but must be further summarised as follows: — She rose at six, awaiting her first summons, which generally came at half-past seven, after the Queen's hair had been dressed by Mrs. Thielky, her wardrobe-woman. Then, with Mrs. Thielky's aid, she dresses the Queen, Mrs. Thielky's office being to hand Fanny the things as they are required, — a fortunate detail, since, as she says, she might run "a prodigious risk of giving the gown before the hoop, or the fan before the neckerchief." By eight the dressing is ended, and the Queen, with the King and Princesses, proceeds to the King's Chapel to prayers, while Fanny goes to breakfast, dawdling meanwhile over a book — for the moment, Gilpin's *Observations* on the Lake District, which Mrs. Delany has lent her. At nine she meditates upon her next immediate business, which generally resolves itself into questions of costume. This done, she is generally her own mistress until a quarter to twelve, occupying the time, if it be not absorbed by the aforesaid questions of costume, in writing or walking. At a quarter before one the Queen usually dresses for the day, when Mrs. Schwellenberg, as well as the "inferior priestesses," is present. The Queen is powdered by her hairdresser, during which time she reads the newspaper. "When she observes that I have run to her but half dressed, she constantly gives me leave to return and finish as soon as she is seated. If she is grave, and reads steadily on, she dismisses me, whether I am dressed or not; but at all times she never forgets to send me away while she is powdering, with a consideration not to spoil my clothes, that one would not expect belonged to her high station. Neither does she ever detain me without making a point of reading some little paragraph aloud."

After a short time Fanny is again summoned, and her further attendance, transferred to the state dressing-room ("if any room in this private mansion can have the epithet of state"), lasts until about three, after which she sees no more of the Queen until bed-time. At five, dinner *en tête-à-tête* with Mrs. Schwellenberg follows in the eating-room, after which coffee in that lady's apartment takes until eight. At eight, descent once more to the eating-room, when the Equerry in Waiting, together with any friend invited by the King or Queen, arrives for tea, which takes till nine. "From that time," — continues Fanny — "if Mrs. Schwellenberg is alone, I never quit her for a minute till I come to my little supper at near eleven. Between eleven and twelve my last summons usually takes place, earlier and later occasionally. Twenty minutes is the customary time then spent with the Queen: half an hour, I believe, is seldom exceeded. I then come back and after doing whatever I can to forward my dress for the next morning, I go to bed — and to sleep, too, believe me: the early rising, and a long day's attention to new affairs and occupations, cause a fatigue so bodily, that nothing mental stands against it, and to sleep I fall the moment I have put out my candle and laid down my head." To these details, it is only necessary to add that the summonses in question were made by a bell (which seems at first to have given Fanny a good deal of annoyance) ; and that it was also a part of her duties to mix the Queen's snuff, — a task which she is recorded to have performed extremely well.

From the above account, it may be gathered that attendance on Queen Charlotte was by no means the most onerous of Miss Burney's functions. Occupying chiefly the middle of the day, it could only have been on Wednesdays and Saturdays (when there were special duties) that it extended to more than four hours, besides which Her Majesty seems to have been laudably solicitous, at all times, to spare her new and very untried attendant. But in Fanny's *carte du jour* there is decidedly an "intolerable deal" of Schwellenberg. Six mortal hours of daily intercourse with this estimable lady, in addition to collaborating with her in what Fanny calls "the irksome and quick-returning labours" of the royal toilette, must have been a cruel penance, only made bearable by Mrs. Schwellenberg's frequent absences on sick leave. Had Mrs. Schwellenberg been a Mrs. Delany, it would not have mattered so much. But she was simply a peevish old person of uncertain temper and impaired health, swaddled in the buckram of backstairs etiquette, captious, arrogant, ignorant, and accustomed — like Mrs. Slipslop — to console herself for her servility to her betters by her rudeness to those beneath her. She was blindly devoted to the Royal Family; but of taste and education she had nothing. Novels and romances she professed to regard as " what you call stuff ";[1] and the only book she was known to favour was Josephus, which was "quoted to solve all difficulties." Her chief enthusiasm was for a pair of pet frogs which croaked when she tapped her snuff-box. " When I only go so . . . knock, knock, knock, they croak all what I please," she would cry in an ecstasy ; and she never wearied of dilating upon their " endearing little qualities " and their healthy appetite for the live flies caught for them by M. de Luc. Although she had been a quarter of a century in England, she still spoke a broken jargon, irresistible to the mimic. She was without conversational gifts, yet she could not endure a moment's silence; she was without resources or power of attraction, yet she was furious at the least suspicion of neglect. Moreover, she seems to have lived in perpetual apprehension of obscure impending spasms, which could only be dissipated by cards. And Fanny hated cards. In moments of irritation, the old lady was capable of the meanest petty tyrannies; in her hours of ease, her amiability to her " good Miss Bernar " was as profuse as it was unpalatable. Several of her objectionable acts are narrated in the *Diary ;* but it is needless to recall them; and

[1] In this she probably only slavishly copied her royal Mistress, who (says Miss Burney) "has a settled aversion to almost all novels, and something very near it to almost all novel-writers" (*Diary and Letters,* 1892, ii. 178).

the situation was obviously complicated by a perhaps intelligible jealousy on the part of the elder woman. Years afterwards, when the *Diary* was first published, the Duke of Sussex thought that its writer was " rather hard. on poor old Schwellenberg "; and it is not impossible that Miss Burney may have somewhat heightened her delineation of a character which afforded so many inviting aspects of attack. Yet, though " Cerbera" or "La Présidente " — as Fanny calls her — may not have been as black as she is painted, it would be hopeless to attempt to decorate her with wings; and there can be little doubt that the happiest hours of the Junior Keeper were those when her untuneable colleague was safely laid up in London or Weymouth with the gout.

Fortunately for Miss Burney all her associates were not of the Schwellenberg type. Miss Planta, English teacher to the two elder Princesses; Miss Goldsworthy (familiarly " Goully "), the sub-governess; Mme. la Fite, who read French to the Queen; and Mme. de Luc, the wife of the fly-catcher, were all amiable enough. And several of the successive Equerries in Waiting, if not actually qualified to regale Mrs. Haggerdorn's successor with that " celestial colloquy sublime " to which Lord Macaulay makes reference, were at least English gentlemen, with pleasant idiosyncrasies of their own, not wholly unworthy of study. There was Miss Goldsworthy's brother, Colonel Philip Goldsworthy, a wag in his way, who relates how the King ineffectually endeavoured to make him carouse on barley water after a hard day's hunting; and who gave a dismally picturesque account of winter service in the ill-constructed Queen's Lodge, where there must

have been as many distinct and several draughts as there
are smells in the City of Cologne. There is the " Colonel
Welbred " of the record, — Colonel Fulke Greville, —
quiet, polite and undemonstrative; there is Colonel
Manners, a good-humoured, careless rattle, who says
whatever comes into his head, and thinks he might
manage to sing the 104th Psalm if he could only keep
from running into " God Save the King"; there is
the " Jessamy Bride's " handsome husband, Colonel
Gwyn; there is Major Price; there is the Queen's
Vice Chamberlain, the Hon. Stephen Digby (" Colonel
Fairly "), grave, scrupulous, diffident, gentle, sentimental, and " assiduously attentive in his manners."   He
is at present married to Lord Ilchester's daughter, by
whom he has four children; but is soon to be a widower.
Lastly, absorbing many pages of the record, is " Mr.
Turbulent," otherwise the Rev. Charles de Guiffardière
or Giffardier, the Queen's French reader, a *farceur* of the
first order, who, apparently to indemnify himself for
the penitential monotony of his past relations with
Mrs. Haggerdorn, — a molluscous personage whom he
contemptuously styles " the Oyster," — indulges Miss
Burney with the most fantastic disquisitions, flights
of rodomontade and mock adoration. Macaulay roundly
writes this gentleman down "half witted," which is
too sweeping; while the charitable Croker opines that
he was laughing at Fanny. Miss Burney's own later
verdict upon " Mr. Turbulent " is, that he was " here
and there a little eccentric, but, in the main, merely
good-humoured and high-spirited." [1]

[1] He was, at all events, clever enough to write, in 1798, a *Cours
Élémentaire d'Histoire Ancienne*, a copy of which is exhibited at
Kew. It is dedicated to Queen Charlotte, and was intended for

In thus bringing some of the personages of the *Diary* before the reader, it has naturally been necessary to anticipate. The narrative of Miss Burney's life at Court is excessively minute; and the chronicle, interesting as it may be in its place, does not always concern what is the prime object of this volume, — the story of her life. One of the first things, for instance, which she has to set down — indeed it happened before she had been three weeks in office — is mad Peg Nicholson's attempt on the King's life, an event which, of course, belongs to history. But Miss Burney's pages add to the story some of those vivid minor details which the daughter of Mnemosyne forgets. She shows us the admirable composure of King George amid his terrified and tearful household; she shows him cheerfully insisting on the usual terrace walk with a single equerry, — on the usual evening concert. But " nothing was listened to," — says Miss Burney of this latter, — " scarce a word was spoken; the Princesses wept continually; the Queen, still more deeply struck, could only, from time to time, hold out her hand to the King, and say ' I have you yet.' " To this we may oppose another and more smiling passage. A few days later came the birthday of the little Princess Amelia; and Fanny's account gives a good idea of one of the popular " terracings " above referred to. " It was really a mighty pretty procession," she says. " The little Princess, just turned of three years old, in a robe-coat covered with fine muslin, a dressed close cap,

---

the use of the Princesses. On the title-page the author is described as Minister of the King's French Chapel [in the Middle Court of St. James's Palace], and Prebendary of Salisbury. He was a married man.

white gloves, and a fan, walked on alone and first, highly delighted in the parade, and turning from side to side to see everybody as she passed: for all the terracers stand up against the walls to make a clear passage for the Royal Family, the moment they come in sight." Then followed the pleased King and Queen with the remainder of the Princesses, — the Princess Royal, the Princesses Augusta, Elizabeth, Mary, Sophia, and their attendants; then, at a little distance, Major Price, the Equerry in Waiting, bringing up the rear to keep off the crowd.

Miss Burney was on the terrace with Mrs. Delany, who had been carried in her chair to the foot of the steps. At sight of Fanny's companion, "the King instantly stopped to speak to her. The Queen, of course, and the little Princess, and all the rest, stood still, in their ranks. They talked a good while with the sweet old lady, during which time the King once or twice addressed himself to me. I caught the Queen's eye, and saw in it a little surprise, but by no means any displeasure to see me of the party. The little Princess went up to Mrs. Delany, of whom she is very fond, and behaved like a little angel to her: she then, with a look of enquiry and recollection, slowly, of her own accord, came behind Mrs. Delany to look at me. 'I am afraid,' said I, in a whisper, and stooping down, 'your Royal Highness does not remember me?' What think you was her answer? An arch little smile, and a nearer approach, with her lips pouted out to kiss me. I could not resist so innocent an invitation; but the moment I had accepted it I was half afraid it might seem, in so public a place, an improper liberty; however, there was no help for it. She then took my fan,

and having looked at it on both sides, gravely returned
it to me, saying, ' O, a brown fan!' The King and
Queen then bid her curtsey to Mrs. Delany, which she
did most gracefully, and they all moved on; each of
the Princesses speaking to Mrs. Delany as they passed,
and condescending to curtsey to her companion."

One of the next things related is a royal visit to
Nuneham (Lord Harcourt's), which included excursions
to Oxford and Blenheim. Miss Burney was one of the
party, but — to use a phrase of Horace Walpole — did
not greatly feel the joy of it, owing to the many discomforts and fatigues arising out of the defective
arrangements which had been made for the Royal
Suite. Mrs. Schwellenberg had assured her that she
should "appear for nobody," and the assurance was
very literally carried out. It was in connection with
this Nuneham trip that occurred the incident of the
gown which has so much exercised some of Fanny's
biographers. Just before the visit took place, Mrs.
Schwellenberg informed " Miss Bernar," with much
patronising importance, that she was to have a gown,
as the Queen said she was not rich. Fanny protested
that [like Dogberry] she had two gowns, and did not
need another. " Miss Bernar," said the scandalised
old lady, " I tell you once, when the Queen will give
you a gown, you must be humble, thankful, when
[even if] you are Duchess of Ancaster," — i.e. Mistress
of the Robes. Further, she was not to be allowed to
thank the Queen herself. " When I give you the
gown," added Mrs. Schwellenberg, " I will tell you
when you may make your curtsey " — and then for the
time the disagreeable conversation stopped. It does
not appear that Fanny got her gown in time for

Nuneham, as she went in a Chambéry gauze of her
own. But it is an error to say—as Lord Macaulay
does—that Queen Charlotte's promise was "never
performed," for a few days later, in September, we
find her wearing her "memorable present-gown" in
honour of the birthday of the Princess Royal. It was
"a lilac tabby," we are told; and the King professed to admire it greatly, calling out that "Emily
[*i.e.* the Princess Amelia] should see Miss Burney's
gown now, and she would think her fine enough."
But from a subsequent entry, it appears that it had
been given through Mrs. Schwellenberg, for Miss
Burney refers to the far greater pleasure that she
received from a gift of violets presented to her by the
Queen herself. Lord Macaulay, in his unwillingness
to believe that Miss Burney obtained any "extraordinary benefactions" from Their Majesties, also over-
looked the fact that, both in 1787 and 1788, Miss
Burney received (though always through Mrs. Schwellenberg) New Year's presents from the Queen. On the
first occasion it was "a complete set of very beautiful
white and gold china for tea, and a coffee-pot, tea-pot,
cream-jug, and milk-jug of silver, in forms remarkably
pretty." In 1788 it was a gift of plate.[1]

Life at Court, whether at Kew, Windsor, or London,
was not riotously eventful, and it has often been
described. The usual humdrum routine repeated
itself, diversified only by concerts, birthdays, and

[1] *Diary and Letters*, 1892, ii. 189, 213, 277, 439. Several
writers have pointed out this unaccountable lapse in the
famous *Edinburgh* essay on Madame D'Arblay. It may be
added that another gift from the Queen, a gold watch set
with pearls, is in the possession of Mrs. Chappel of East
Orchard, Shaftesbury.

change of equerries. During much of the latter part
of 1786, Mrs. Schwellenberg was ill, and Fanny
reigned in her stead over the Windsor tea-table.
Early in 1787, the Court went to London, taking up
its abode at St. James's Palace. During this time,
Miss Burney also was occasionally ill, and went home
for change. Once she visited Drury Lane with the
Royal Family; and was startled by a complimentary
reference to herself in the Epilogue to Holcroft's
Seduction — " a very clever piece," — she says, — " but
containing a dreadful picture of vice and dissipation
in high life." The reference was to " sweet *Cecilia*,"

" Whose every passion yields to Reason's laws,"[1] —

and seems to have delighted her Royal Master and
Mistress as much as — we are assured — it embarrassed
and disconcerted herself. " I took a peep at you!"
said the kind King later, — " I could not help that. I
wanted to see how you looked when your father first
discovered your writing — and now I think I know!"
Not very long subsequently, she had a compliment on
the subject of *Cecilia* from another quarter. Mrs.
Siddons, who was staying in the neighbourhood of
Windsor, was ordered to the Lodge to read a play ;
and Fanny was requested by the Queen to receive her.
Almost the first thing the other Queen — the stage
Queen — said to Miss Burney was, that " there was no
part she had ever so much wished to act as that
of Cecilia." Notwithstanding this most conciliatory
speech, Mrs. Siddons — stately and beautiful as she

[1] Miss Burney probably quoted from memory, as the couplet
in the Epilogue to the printed play runs as follows: —

> " And oft let soft *Cecilia* win your praise ;
> While Reason guides the clue, in Fancy's maze."

was — does not appear to have impressed *Cecilia's*
author. " I found her " — says Fanny — " the Heroine
of a Tragedy, — sublime, elevated, and solemn. In
face and person, truly noble and commanding ; in
manners, quiet and stiff ; in voice, deep and dragging ;
and in conversation, formal, sententious, calm and dry.
I expected her to have been all that is interesting ; the
delicacy and sweetness with which she seizes every
opportunity to strike and to captivate upon the stage
had persuaded me that her mind was formed with that
peculiar susceptibility which, in different modes, must
give equal powers to attract and to delight in common
life. But I was very much mistaken." The play Mrs.
Siddons read was Vanbrugh and Cibber's *Provoked
Husband*. As Fanny did not hear it, we have no
account of its effect. But it would be interesting to
know whether the entire absence of applause on these
occasions, which so paralysed the mercurial Garrick,
had the same effect on the majestic Mrs. Siddons.

In this way, what Fanny calls the " dead and tame
life I now lead," — of which the above was one of the
rare variations, — went on as before, although there are
signs in her Journal now and then, that it was sometimes less irksome to her. Indeed, on one occasion
she goes so far as to write that she has now thoroughly
formed her mind to her situation. " I even think "
— she adds — " I now should do ill to change it ; for
though my content with it has been factitious, I
believe it, in the main, suited to save me from more
disturbance than it gives me." With ampler space, it
would be easy to fill a considerable number of pages
by the vagaries of " Mr. Turbulent," the divers
humours of the equerries, and the whims of Mrs.

Schwellenberg, who vacillates between endeavouring to kill her colleague by making her sit in a draught of a carriage window, and to conciliate her by the premature legacy of a sedan chair. But in the limits assigned to this chapter we can only hope to chronicle the more important events.

One of these was the trial of Warren Hastings, which began in February, 1788, in Westminster Hall. The Queen gave Fanny two tickets for the box of the Grand Chamberlain (Sir Peter Burrell), where she was just above the prisoner, whose pale and harassed face she could see distinctly with her glass when he looked up. Concerning the "high crimes and misdemeanours" alleged against him, she knew nothing, regarding the whole matter "as a party affair." But her sympathies, like those of the Royal Household, were provisionally with Hastings, whom she had met two years earlier at the Cambridges at Twickenham, and had liked, — circumstances which she found somewhat embarrassing when presently she saw her other friend, Burke, with knit brows and scroll in hand, making portentous entry at the head of the Committee for the Prosecution. Great part of the first day's proceedings was taken up by the interminably tedious over-reading of the charges; but Mr. Windham, one of the Committee, and her sister Charlotte's neighbour in Norfolk,[1]

---

[1] Charlotte Burney was by this time married to Clement Francis, a surgeon practising at Aylsham, about five miles from Windham's seat at Felbrigge. Mrs. Ellis, quoting from "a family account," says "Clement Francis had been Secretary to Warren Hastings in India, and while there he read, and was so charmed with *Evelina*, that he was seized with a desire to make the authoress his wife, and, with that intent, came home from India and obtained an introduction to Dr. Burney and

speedily asked to be presented to her; and, from
time to time, visited the Grand Chamberlain's box,
pointing out the different notabilities, — among the rest,
Hastings' arch-enemy, Philip Francis. Mr. Windham,
who was a man of the world and a brilliant talker,
made himself extremely agreeable, though he was probably not so convincingly impressed by Miss Burney's
instinctive conviction of the innocence of the late
Governor General of Bengal as she imagined. A
little later, she went again to Westminster Hall to
hear Burke, her companion upon this occasion being
her brother James. It was the second day of Burke's
speech, — the first she had not heard. What she did
hear surpassed her expectations; and what she says
is confirmed by other auditors of that splendid oratory.
She notes its inequality, — its digressions. But, she
goes on — not without a touch of the Johnsonian
" triptology " — " when he narrated, he was easy,
flowing and natural; when he declaimed, energetic,
warm and brilliant. The sentiments he interspersed
were as nobly conceived as they were highly coloured;
his satire had a poignancy of wit that made it as entertaining as it was penetrating; his allusions and quotations, as far as they were English and within my reach,
were apt and ingenious; and the wild and sudden
flights of his fancy, bursting forth from his creative
imagination in language fluent, forcible, and varied,
had a charm for my ear and my attention wholly new
and perfectly irresistible." In fact, she continues,
" the whirlwind of his eloquence nearly drew me into
its vortex." Upon a third occasion, she heard Charles

his family, but the result was that he married the younger
sister — Charlotte" (*Early Diary*, 1889, ii. 273 n.).

Fox raging for five hours at the Lords, who, in the opinion of the Committee, were favouring the accused. But Fanny thought Fox's face looked hard and callous, and that Burke's method of speaking was more gentleman-like, scholar-like, and fraught with true genius than that of Fox. On each of these visits, it should be added, she had much talk with Mr. Windham, who, for further recommendation, had been one of Johnson's devotees; and she made careful report of her impressions to Queen Charlotte.

Another person to whom her accounts of the first scenes of the Great Trial had been specially welcome was now soon to be lost to her. On the 15th of April, 1788, not long after the above events, died Mrs. Delany. Her death was a serious blow to Fanny, who had resorted to her freely for sympathy when things went wrong either with the Senior Keeper, or in the "nice conduct" of the Equerries' tea-table. In the July following, the King, whose health had hitherto been of the best, showed the first indications of that malady which was afterwards to be of so serious a character. As a consequence, it was decided that, in company with the Queen and the three elder Princesses, he should go to Cheltenham to drink the waters, — carrying with him the Royal household in concentrated form. Fanny and Miss Planta were of the party; Colonel Gwyn was the Equerry in Waiting; and Colonel Digby attended in his capacity of Queen's Vice-Chamberlain. They were domiciled at Fauconberg Hall (Bay's Hill Lodge), which was charmingly situated, but ridiculously restricted in point of accommodation. At Cheltenham, King George repeated his usual simple life, promenading daily in the Walks to the delight of

M

the lieges; and from time to time making flying visits
in the neighbourhood from which Miss Planta and
Miss Burney were, of necessity, excluded.   One result
of these proceedings was to throw Miss Burney very
much into the society of Colonel Digby, now a recently
bereft and melancholy widower with a young family.
The Queen's Vice-Chamberlain was ten years older
than Miss Burney; and rumour was already connecting
his name with that of his eventual second wife, Miss
Charlotte Gunning, a pretty Maid of Honour, who
figures in the *Diary* as "Miss Fuzelier," and was the
eldest daughter of a baronet.   Meanwhile, in the contracted limits of Bay's Hill Lodge, both Colonel Digby
and Miss Burney — like fellow-sufferers upon a raft —
seem to have discovered that they had much in common.
They exchanged ideas upon many subjects, staidly
discussing religion and the affections, and particularly
the second volume of a work with the "injudicious"
title of *Original Love Letters*.[1]   Fanny was admittedly
much "flattered" by the Colonel's attraction to her little
parlour; and in her *Diary* the record of this pleasant
oasis in her pilgrimage has all the aspect of a decorous
sentimental idyll.   Unhappily, practical confirmation
of the doleful Colonel's standing topic — "the assured
misery of all stations and all seasons in this vain and
restless world" — arrived suddenly with a fit of the gout.
This effectually put a stop to any further study of
Akenside's *Odes* and Falconer's *Shipwreck;* and on the
8th of August Colonel Digby was forced to obtain sick

[1] This was by the copious William Combe, author of
Dr. Syntax.   The full title is — *Original Love Letters, between a
Lady of Quality and a Person of Inferior Condition,* Dublin,
1794, two vols.

leave, and departed. Almost immediately afterwards, and not entirely without Fanny's good offices, — he was appointed to the vacant Mastership of St. Catherine's Hospital, a sinecure in the Queen's gift. With this, what Fanny styles, in a double sense, "the Cheltenham episode" drew to an end; and the Royal Household went back to the "set, gray life" of old. To make matters worse, before a few weeks were over, the King was again indisposed. In October those about him were vaguely uneasy; and in the night of the 20th, he was alarmingly ill. This attack however passed off; and on the 25th the Court moved from Kew to Windsor. On that day Miss Burney had "a sort of conference" with the King, which she explains to mean that she "was the object to whom he spoke." Though he was as gracious and kind as usual, she was shocked at the hoarseness, volubility, and even vehemence of his speech. The next day she met him again in the passage from the Queen's room. "He stopped me, and conversed upon his health near half an hour, still with that extreme quickness of speech and manner that belongs to fever; and he hardly sleeps, he tells me, one minute all night; indeed, if he recovers not his rest, a most delirious fever seems to threaten him. He is all agitation, all emotion, yet all benevolence and goodness, even to a degree that makes it touching to hear him speak. He assures everybody of his health; he seems only fearful to give uneasiness to others, yet certainly he is better than last night. Nobody speaks of his illness, nor what they think of it."

For the next few days, notwithstanding that the King seemed sometimes better than at other times, he grew steadily worse. He became appreciably weaker; he walked like a gouty man; he had talked away all his voice, and his hoarseness was pitiful to hear. Nevertheless he was as amiable as ever: — "he seemed to have no anxiety but to set the Queen at rest, and no wish but to quiet and give pleasure to all around him." In the meantime the poor Queen is overcome with nameless apprehension; walks up and down the room without uttering a word, shaking her head in manifest distress and irresolution. So matters wear on until the 3rd November when Dr. Heberden is called in, "for counsel [it is announced], not that His Majesty is worse." Yet on the following day the Queen is in deeper distress than before; the King is in a state almost incomprehensible; and all the household is uneasy and alarmed. On the 5th, His Majesty goes out for an airing with the Princess Royal; and the Prince of Wales arrives from Brighton. Then between six and seven, an inexplicable stillness comes upon the Upper Lodge, as if something had happened. No one stirs; no one speaks. The evening concert is stopped. The equerries are gloomy and uncommunicative, though it is vaguely understood that the King is much worse, and that the Queen herself has been taken ill. At last Miss Burney learns the truth from the Vice-Chamberlain. At dinner His Majesty had broken into a positive fit of delirium, and the Queen had been in violent hysterics. "All the Princesses were in misery, and the Prince of Wales had burst into tears.[1] No one knew what was to follow — no one could conjecture the event."

---

[1] Not of pity, but of fear. According to his own after-account at Lord Jersey's table, the King, under some sudden impatience of control, had seized him by the collar, and thrust him violently against the wall.

What did follow has been told and retold, and much of it belongs to history. But Miss Burney's *Diary* reveals the domestic details of the story as it is not recorded in the periods of the politician, or in the professional evidence of the doctors. She depicts the wearing suspense of the household, the confusion and clash of conjectures, the grief and agony of the Queen, the waiting rooms and passages filled with silent pages and attendants, the thick, depressing November fog, the hoarse voice of the King, talking, talking, talking incessantly, — but still breathing nothing but consideration for those about him.[1] Then comes, by order of the physicians, to whom a third has now been added, the separation of the wife and husband. This was on the 6th. On the morning of the next day Miss Burney hears the Prince of Wales tell the Queen what had happened the night before. The King had got up, and insisted upon going into the next room, which to his amazement, he found crowded with members of the household ranged in dead silence around it on chairs and sofas. He inquired what they did there, spoke fondly of his favourite son, the Duke of York (then present, but not seen) and finally penned Sir George Baker [the Queen's physician] into a corner, calling him an old woman, who did not understand his complaint, which was only nervous. During all this, no one dared approach him. At last Colonel Digby (who, in his own family, had some experience of demented persons) took him by the arm, and begged him to go back to bed. The King refused,

---

[1] "Upon one occasion he is said to have talked unceasingly for sixteen hours" (*Auckland Correspondence*, ii. 244, quoted in Jesse's *Life and Reign of George III.*, 1867, iii. 58).

and asked him who he was. "I am Colonel Digby, Sir"—he answered—"and your Majesty has been very good to me often, and now I am going to be very good to you, for you must come to bed, Sir, it is necessary to your life." The King was so surprised that he let himself be drawn away like a child.

In the fortnight that followed, things passed from bad to worse for the dwellers in the Upper Lodge. To add to the general disquiet and apprehension, Mrs. Schwellenberg arrived from Weymouth "all spasm and horror." Then, by order of the Prince of Wales, intercourse with the outer world was practically suspended. As the King's condition did not alter, the physicians told Mr. Pitt plainly that his ailment was lunacy; and on the 28th it was decided that he should be transferred to Kew, a place he detested, but where it was possible for him to take exercise without observation. Accordingly, on that day, the Queen and Princesses made precipitate and miserable exodus to Kew, amid the tears of the sorrowing household,— even the sentinels crying bitterly as they looked on. Then came the difficult task of persuading the King to follow, which he eventually did, being induced thereto by the promise that he should see the Queen,—a promise which was not kept, with the result that the night which ensued was one of the most violently bad of any yet passed. And so, "in all its dark colours, dark as its darkest prognostics," began the "Kew campaign" from which, as usual, Mrs. Schwellenberg was not absent.

To recapitulate the discomforts of the cold and carpetless building at Kew, never intended for a winter residence, and lacking sadly both in space and

accommodation, is here needless. But, notwithstanding Miss Burney's "darkest prognostics," a brighter
day was happily dawning. New doctors were added to
the old; and the new were better. Dr. Francis Willis
and his son, both of whom had special experience in
mental disease, henceforth, and much to the satisfaction
of the household, took practical charge of the case.
Honest, open, cheerful and high-minded, their moral
influence over their patient, in combination with a
gentler and more humane method of treatment, was
not slow to produce its effect. The King began to
walk regularly in the gardens; and hopes of his
recovery fitfully revived. But while his health vacil-
lated, the world outside was agitating for a Regency.
The Willises — of whom there were now three —
persevered no less with their regimen. And so, —
omitting many immaterial things, — we come to the
2nd February, a day memorable in Fanny's annals.
For the sake of her health, she had been advised to
walk daily either at Richmond or at Kew, according
to the report she received of the King's whereabouts.
On this particular day, she had been told that His
Majesty would walk in Richmond Park, and she
therefore directed her steps to Kew Gardens. It
had been arranged that if, on any occasion, the King
chanced to see her, she was to be allowed to run off.
By some misapprehension, he *was* in the Gardens, and
at once detected her presence. What was worse, she
soon heard him hurrying after her, calling hoarsely
"Miss Burney! Miss Burney!" Terrified beyond
measure, she continued to run until she was peremp-
torily bidden to stop by the Willises, as His Majesty
was doing himself harm. "When they were within

a few yards of me," she writes, "the King called out,
'Why did you run away?'" Making a violent effort
to regain her composure, she turned to meet him,
when to her astonishment, the poor invalid, with " all
his wonted benignity," despite the wildness still in his
eyes, put both his hands round her shoulders, and
kissed her on the cheek, going on to exhibit such
delight at seeing her again, that she straightway
lost all her fear. A long, disconnected conversation
ensued. He rallied her about Mrs. Schwellenberg.
She was not to mind: he (King George) was her
friend. He talked about the pages; about her father;
about Handel, some passages of whose Oratorios he
tried to sing — hoarsely. He spoke also, with tears
in his eyes, of Mrs. Delany. At length, after repeated
injunctions on the part of his medical attendants, he
let her go — his last words being to reassure her upon
the subject of Mrs. Schwellenberg. All this — some of
the Schwellenberg part excepted — Fanny recounted
faithfully to the Queen on her return.

Not long after, the King's state began to amend,
greatly to the dismay of the advocates of the Regency
Bill. Before that measure could be read a third
time, he was almost himself again; and at the end of
February was able personally to assure Miss Burney
of his convalescent condition. She found him in the
Queen's dressing room, where he had waited on
purpose to see her. "I am quite well now " — he
said; "I was nearly so when I saw you before — but
I could overtake you better now." Ten days later,
at the time of the general rejoicing, when the Queen
had had a special transparency painted for Kew Palace
by her favourite Biagio Rebecca, the little Princess

Amelia led her father to the front window to see the illuminations, dropping first upon her knees with a copy of congratulatory verses, which had been expressly composed for the occasion by the Junior Keeper of Robes. Miss Burney was as "ill at these numbers" as most manufacturers of metrical loyalty; but her postscript

> "The little bearer begs a kiss
> From dear Papa, for bringing this " —

was naturally not spoken in vain. On the next day the King, reinstated in all his dignities, received, in person, the Address of the Lords and Commons upon his restoration to health.

Over the further progress of that restoration we may pass rapidly. By this date, March 11th, 1789, Miss Burney had been more than two years and a half in the Queen's service, and her stay was to be prolonged for two years more. But it is needless to pursue its story with equal detail. After the Royal Family quitted Kew, they went to Weymouth, their progress to that watering-place being one continued scene of loyal and very genuine rejoicing. At Weymouth, where they were domiciled in Gloucester House, Miss Burney renewed her acquaintance with Mrs. Siddons, whom she saw as Rosalind, but considered "too large for that shepherd's dress," and as Lady Townly in the *Provoked Husband* which she had read at Windsor. Fanny thought her gaiety was only gravity disguised, and though she praises her as Cibber's heroine, evidently preferred the "great Sarah" of the Georgian Era in tragedy. She also, and for the first time, beheld Mr. Pitt; but did not

admire his appearance, which she affirms was neither
noble nor expressive. She spent much of her time
with the beautiful "Jessamy Bride," Mrs. Gwyn; and
among other places, visited the Plymouth Dockyard,
describing the forging of an anchor there with something of that later fine writing which was so effectually
to ruin her style. " While we were seeing the anchor
business, which seemed performed by Vulcanic demons,
so black they looked, so savage was their howl in
striking the red-hot iron, and so coarse and slight
their attire " — is quite in the perverse manner of the
coming *Memoirs of Dr. Burney.* In returning from
Weymouth, the Royal party stopped at Longleat,
which gives her an opportunity of moralising, — in
Bishop Ken's bedroom, — upon the cruelty of Longleat's
former tenant, " Granville the polite," in forcing her
old friend Mrs. Delany, to marry *en premières noces,*
that extremely undesirable suitor, Mr. Pendarves of
Roscrow. And so, by Tottenham Park, where the
Earl of Aylesbury had put up a new bed for the King
and Queen which cost him £900, they got back to
Windsor in September. At this date the King had
completely lost all traces of his indisposition.

Once again at Windsor, the Court sank back into
its old jog-trot tedium, and with it sank Fanny's
heart. There was now no Mrs. Delany to sympathise
when Schwellenbergism reached a more acute stage
than usual; and there was shortly to be no Colonel
Digby with whom to deplore the vicissitudes of a vale
of tears, or to discuss, "in his genteel roundabout
way," the improving *Night Thoughts* of Dr. Young.
Colonel Digby, who, from time to time, had renewed
at Windsor the old readings, tea-drinkings, and semi-

confidential conversations, had not taken a very prominent part in the Weymouth expedition. But he had
apparently been permitting himself other distractions;
and about November his connection with the Court
was interrupted by his approaching marriage to
Miss Gunning, with whom — and even by the King
during his insanity — his name, as we have said, had
already been associated. There is no doubt that
Miss Burney had been impressed by him, if only
as the most refined and amiable of her colleagues;
and there can also be no doubt that on his part he
must have found her sympathy and companionship
especially grateful in his newly bereaved condition.
However this may be — and Miss Burney could not
have behaved better if she had been Cecilia herself —
this last event manifestly added its quota to the
growing burden of her life; and it was not in her
nature to conceal her discomforts, either mental or
physical. Her health declined visibly; the Schwellenberg card-table grew more wearisome than ever; and
her condition began to cause anxiety to her friends.
At last she took advantage of an accident to speak
frankly to her father. She told him plainly that,
kind and considerate as were the King and Queen,
the situation had grown insupportable; and that
she "could never, in any part of the live-long day,
command liberty, or social intercourse, or repose." [1]

---

[1] At a later date she puts the matter in a nutshell. " I am
inexpressibly grateful to the Queen, but I burn to be delivered
from Mrs. Schwellenberg." She argued, and argued justly,
that, unless the desire of further intercourse was reciprocal,
she ought only to belong to Mrs. Schwellenberg officially, and
at official hours. But " Cerbera " was an old and faithful
servant of the Royal Family ; and it was obviously difficult

Dr. Burney himself had for some time not been wholly happy about her position; and he of course opened his arms to her return. But he was not rich, and he was manifestly so much upset at the thought of her retirement that, for the moment, the matter was allowed to drop.

Meanwhile the months once more rolled on monotonously. To divert her thoughts, she took up a tragedy which she had begun during the King's illness; and the rumour that she had again her pen in hand — upon a satirical novel, as it was supposed — sent a flutter of apprehension through the Windsor dove-cotes. Her friends continued to carry dismal accounts to London of her failing condition, and loudly exclaimed against Dr. Burney's irresolution. Walpole asked whether her talents were given to be buried in obscurity. Windham, whom she saw occasionally during the further dilatory progress of the Hastings trial, threatened to set the Literary Club on her father, who was a member of that community. Busybody Boswell — another member — also interested himself (not perhaps without ulterior views of his own as regards her Johnson material) in her behalf. "We shall address Dr. Burney in a body," he said; and then he asked her to give him some of Dr. Johnson's "choice little notes," — a request she with difficulty evaded. At last a joint Memorial was drawn up by Dr. Burney and his daughter, praying that she might be permitted to resign, and it was arranged to put it forward on the most favourable

to explain the state of affairs to Her Majesty, one of whose objects moreover had been to give Mrs. Schwellenberg a pleasant companion in her old age.

opportunity. But the opportunity did not arise, and still time went on. She grew worse, having constantly, in the course of the obnoxious card parties, to crawl to her room for hartshorn and a few moments of rest. By and by the presentation of the memorial grew imperative. To the horror of Mrs. Schwellenberg, for whom such a proceeding was sheer self-destruction, it was hesitatingly handed in. The Queen, to whom it is difficult to believe that the matter was wholly unexpected, was visibly surprised and disturbed. She, however, expressed the hope that a long holiday might set Miss Burney right. But with this Miss Burney's father — now thoroughly alive to the exigencies of the case, — could not agree; and to Her Majesty's disappointment, and the unconcealed disgust of Mrs. Schwellenberg, it was decided she must go. When her departure was definitely settled, a Martin's summer seems to have followed, in which even "Cerbera" softened somewhat — admitting, in her favourite phrase, that "The Bernan bin reely agribble." Fanny had a short illness, which helped to strengthen her case; and then, in July, 1791, five years after she had entered the Upper Lodge, she quitted it for ever, being too much affected to bid her royal Master a final farewell.

Much ink has been expended on that portion of Fanny Burney's career which forms the subject of this chapter. Exceptionally clever and gifted she was, without doubt; but with all her abilities, it must be admitted that, neither by her antecedents nor her experiences, was she suited for the post she was called upon to fill. The merely mechanical part of it she might perhaps have acquired, — though it

seems she never did. Etiquette and formality she
heartily detested; she was unmethodical; she was negli-
gent in her dress ; she was not always (in the presentation of petitions and the like) entirely judicious and
tactful.   Nevertheless, there is nothing to show that,
save for the death of Mrs. Delany, the terrible tension
of the King's illness, the defection of Colonel Digby,
and, above all, the unrelieved infliction of Mrs. Schwellenberg's company and caprices, — the " one flaw " in her
lot, she calls it, — she might not gradually have grown
reconciled to her court life.   If she were not (and it
was no shame to her!) as good a Queen's Dresser as
Mrs. Haggerdorn, she was certainly — although, perhaps
from her weak voice and short sight, she practically
failed- as a reader — an infinitely better " Confidential
Companion."   The " Oyster " would have been utterly
incompetent to report the Hastings trial, or to scribble
a royal copy of verses to the Master of the Horse, or to
delight the Queen by a circumstantial and picturesque
account of the interview with the King in the gardens
at Kew.   And whatever Miss Burney's dislike may have
been to one or two of her colleagues, her own personal
good qualities and intellectual capacity were always
cordially recognised by all the Royal Family.[1]   As
to the enforced suspension of her literary labours, not
only is that a grievance which she herself never felt
or advanced ; but when she came to Windsor in 1786,
she had absolutely written nothing for four years.
Nor were there any indications that she was likely
to write anything.   Her most stimulating friend and

---

[1] This appreciation she never lost. She speaks of herself later
as " having resigned royal service without resigning royal
favour " (Diary and Letters, 1892, iv. 7).

critic, "Daddy" Crisp, was dead; and she professed, or affected to profess (like a greater writer after *The Newcomes*),[1] that her vein had run dry with her latest book. Moreover, we now know what her first critics did not know, namely, that so far from receiving two thousand pounds for *Cecilia*, she had only — after more than a year's hard work — received two hundred and fifty pounds. The deserts of genius are not easily assessed; but looking to all the circumstances, those who, in this particular instance, regarded two hundred a year for life, with accommodation and other advantages, as an offer worth considering by a diffident and delicate woman of four and thirty, whose entire gains by two popular novels, making eight volumes, had not exceeded two hundred and eighty pounds — can scarcely be said to have been wholly unwise in their generation. That there would be compensating drawbacks of tedium and restraint, they no doubt expected; but that the accidents of the employment would make the post untenable, was a result they could not possibly foresee.

[1] "I have exhausted all the types of character with which I am familiar" — Thackeray told the Rev. Whitwell Elwin in 1856. "I can't jump further than I did in *The Newcomes*" (*Some XVIIIᵗʰ Century Men of Letters*, 1903, i. 156).

CHAPTER VII

HALF A LIFETIME

WHATEVER view may be taken of the effect of Miss Burney's life at Court upon her literary prospects, it was allowed by King George that she had sacrificed something. "It is but her due," said that amiable monarch, referring to the Queen's intention of granting her late Keeper of Robes a retiring allowance. "She has given up five years of her pen." A hundred pounds per annum may not, it is true, seem much; but considering the amount of Miss Burney's salary, and the brief duration of her service, it was not illiberal. And it came out of the Queen's pocket. "It is solely from *me* to *you*," — Her Majesty told her, adding other friendly expressions of farewell. This pension, or retiring allowance, — as far as we know, — Miss Burney continued to receive for the greater part of her life, which lasted forty-eight years more. That this is also the period comprised in the present chapter, may appear — at first sight — to suggest a certain hurry at the close. But the fault lies with the material, not with the limits of the volume. After Miss Burney's resignation, and her marriage two years later, the events of her career, as well as the record of them, grow less interesting. She wrote tragedies, one of which was produced, and

176

failed. She wrote a comedy, which was never produced at all. She wrote — mainly for money — two
novels, which were commercial successes but added
nothing to her reputation. Finally, in extreme old
age, she wrote *Memoirs* of her father, which have
been over-abused, but which cannot conscientiously
be praised. Such are the leading facts of her literary
life from the 7th July, 1791, — the day she quitted
St. James's Palace, — to her death in 1840.

For a week or two she remained at home, — home
being now Chelsea College, where her father was
domiciled. Then her kind friend, Mrs. Ord, carried her
off on a four months' tour to recruit. " She rambled "
— in Macaulay's picturesque phrases — " by easy jour-
neys from cathedral to cathedral, and from watering-
place to watering-place. She crossed the New Forest,
and visited Stonehenge and Wilton, the cliffs of Lyme,
and the beautiful valley of Sidmouth. Thence she
journeyed by Powderham Castle, and by the ruins of
Glastonbury Abbey, to Bath, and from Bath, when
the winter was approaching, returned well and cheerful to London."[1] By this time it was the middle of
October. Her father had anxiously awaited her
coming, not without hope that she would forthwith
resume her literary pursuits. Resume them indeed
she did, but fitfully, working chiefly at tragedies, two
of which she had roughly sketched at Windsor. To
these she now added a third. "I go on with various
writings," she says at the close of 1791, "at different
times, and just as the humour strikes. I have promised
my dear father a Christmas Box, and a New Year's
gift upon my return from Norbury Park, and therefore

[1] *Edinburgh Review*, January 1843, lxxvi. 557.

N

he now kindly leaves me to my own devices." But
social functions, as in the post-Cecilian days, began to
exercise their old attraction; and, in her *Diary*, we
frequently trace her at places which were not those
haunts of study and imagination, the great and little
" Grubberies " at Chelsea. She visits poor Sir Joshua,
now nearly blind, with bandaged and green-shaded
eyes, and fast nearing his end.[1] " ' I am very glad,'
he said, in a meek voice and dejected accent, ' to see
you again, and I wish I could see you better! but I
have only one eye now — and hardly that.' " She visits
Buckingham House periodically, and even looks in
upon " Cerbera," who is unexpectedly cordial, though
she has evidently not forgiven her old colleague for
declining to die at her post. During the temporary
lameness of her successor, Mlle. Jacobi, Miss Burney
goes so far as to resume her attendance for two days,
only to be amply assured, by that brief experience, of
the peril she has escaped. " Indeed," — she says, —
" I was half dead with only two days' and nights' exer-
tion." She goes again to the ever-during Hastings
trial,[2] renewing her relations with Windham; she goes
to a public breakfast at Mrs. Montagu's in Portman
Square, and sees the Feather Room, referred to in
chapter iv. " It was like a full Ranelagh by day-
light," she writes; and among other guests she meets
Sophy Streatfield, no longer the peerless " S.S." of
yore, but faded, and sad, and changed. Another visit
she mentions is to Mrs. Crewe at Hampstead. Mrs.
Crewe, it will be remembered, was the daughter of

[1] Sir Joshua Reynolds died on the 23rd February following.
[2] One of the tickets given to her by the Queen is preserved by
Archdeacon Burney of Surbiton.

Fanny's godmother, Mrs. Greville. Here she listens
to Burke's praise of her dead friend, Mrs. Delany,
whom he affirms to have been "a real fine lady"—
"the model of an accomplished woman of former
times"; and she reads with her hostess the newly
published *Pleasures of Memory* of Mr. Samuel Rogers.

The close of 1792 was saddened by the sudden death
of Miss Burney's brother-in-law, Mr. Francis of Aylsham, — an event which detained her for some time in
Norfolk. It is about this time, too, that we begin to
hear of the French refugees whose arrival in this country, previous to the execution of Louis the Sixteenth,
was to exercise so important an influence upon Fanny's
fortunes. The letters of Mrs. Phillips from Mickleham
are much occupied with these illustrious exiles. There
is the Duc de Liancourt, who has escaped to England
in a small boat covered with faggots; there is Mme.
de Broglie, who has taken a little cottage hard by in
the hamlet of West Humble. There is a group who
have clubbed to rent Juniper Hall — a delightful and
still existent house on the road between Mickleham
and Burford Bridge. This group, or syndicate, consists of Count Louis de Narbonne, ex-Minister of War;
of the Marquise de la Châtre and her son; of M. de
Montmorency, "a *ci-devant Duc*"; of M. de Jaucourt;
and afterwards of Mme. de Staël, and M. Ch. Maurice
de Talleyrand-Périgord, late Bishop of Autun, — not
yet the terrible old man of Maclise's sketch and Ros-
setti's scathing description,[1] but a dignified personage of
eight-and-thirty. Finally there was M. de Narbonne's
friend, M. Alexandre D'Arblay, an artillery officer,

[1] In an article in the *Academy* for 15th April, 1871, on the Maclise Gallery in *Fraser's Magazine*.

maréchal de camp and former adjutant-general to La
Fayette. On the night of the flight to Varennes he
had been on guard at the Tuileries. With all these
pathetic figures of exile, the waif and stray of a fallen
Constitution, Mrs. Phillips, with her French traditions
and education, was delighted; but particularly with
the last. "He seems to me" — she writes to Fanny in
November — "a true *militaire, franc et loyal* — open as
the day — warmly affectionate to his friends — intelligent, ready, and amusing in conversation, with a great
share of *gaieté de cœur*, and at the same time, of *naïveté*
and *bonne foi.*" Further, he was announced to be about
forty, tall, with a good figure, and a frank and manly
countenance. Like his friend, Narbonne, he had lost
almost everything, but what Narbonne had left they
were to share. "Quoique ce soit, nous le partagerons
ensemble," he said. "Je ne m'en fais pas le moindre
scrupule, puisque nous n'avons eu qu'un intérêt com-
mun, et nous nous sommes toujours aimés comme
frères."

Early in January, having duly presented herself at
Buckingham House on the Queen's Birthday, Fanny
set out for Norbury Park, arriving just after the news
of the execution of Louis the Sixteenth, an event
which of course overwhelmed her. With her quick
sympathies, she was soon absorbed by the interesting
tenants of *Junipère*, as they called it; and they, on
their side, were equally interested in the author of
Cecilia.[1] Mme. de Staël, who was now at the head
of the little French colony, was especially amiable to
the lady whom she designates "la première femme

---

[1] *Cecilia*, it may be mentioned, had been translated at Neuchâtel
in 1783.

d'Angleterre"; and Fanny seems to have been delighted from the first with Narbonne and his friend. M. D'Arblay — she tells her father — "is one of the most delightful characters I have ever met, for openness, probity, intellectual knowledge, and unhackneyed manners." Very soon she is being pressed by Mme. de Staël — who is as ardent as Mrs. Thrale — to come and stay at Juniper. Concurrently, M. D'Arblay, who, in addition to his other good qualities, turns out to be "passionately fond of literature, a most delicate critic in his own language, well versed in both Italian and German, and a very elegant poet,"[1] undertakes to teach her French in return for lessons in English. Dr. Burney, who received these confidences (*per* favour of M. de Talleyrand *en route* to his too expensive lodgings in Woodstock Street), and no doubt recollected the similar relations of Sir Charles Grandison and Clementina, must have foreseen the result — not without misgiving. He did not like Talleyrand; there was gossip afloat about Narbonne and Mme. de Staël; and at length, when "this enchanting M. D'Arblay" (as Fanny calls him to Mrs. Locke) openly expressed what was no doubt a genuine affection for his daughter, he was naturally averse from a match which promised so little, as the gentleman had no prospect of regaining his lost fortune, and Fanny had only her pension and her pen. But romance, and the world, were, as usual, against common sense; and after retreating for a little "maiden meditation" to Chessington, whither she was promptly

---

[1] He was, indeed, a better poet than Fanny herself, to judge from some graceful *vers d'occasion*, printed in the *Diary*, which he addressed to her on her birthday. The quatrain he placed under her portrait is not so happy.

followed by her lover, Fanny was eventually married to
M. D'Arblay at Mickleham Church on the 31st July,
1793, Captain Burney, in the absence of his father,
giving her away. Owing to the bridegroom's being a
Roman Catholic, the ceremony was, on the following day,
repeated at the chapel of the Sardinian Ambassador
in London — the object being that, if by any chance
M. D'Arblay came to his own again, his wife might
not be debarred from participation. Their means for
the present were limited to Fanny's pension, which, it
had been feared, might be withdrawn. This fear,
however, must have been removed. Mr. Locke gave
them a site for a cottage in Norbury Park, adding
cheerfully that after all, £100 per annum was but the
income of many curates. But the view of the out-
siders is expressed by Miss Maria Josepha Holroyd
in a letter to her friend Miss Firth. "I must desire
you " — she writes — "to wonder at Miss Burney's marriage if I have not mentioned it before. She met with
Monsieur D'Arblay at Mr. Locke's, therefore probably
Mme. de Staël was in the secret." . . . "He [M.
D'Arblay] is even worse off than many other Emigrants,
who have at least a futurity of Order in France to look
forward to. But this man is disinherited by his father,
for the part he took in politics, having followed La-
Fayette on his État Major. Miss Burney has nothing
but the 100*l* from the Queen. Should you not have
formed a better opinion of the author of *Cecilia* ?"[1]

---

[1] *The Girlhood of Maria Josepha Holroyd* (Lady Stanley of
Alderley), 1897, 2nd edn. pp. 229–30. Mrs. Barrett (*Diary
and Letters*, 1892, iv. 476) puts the income "for a considerable
time " at about £125, so that it must have been supplemented in
some way.

The match, not the less, was a thoroughly happy one. "Never," — says Mme. D'Arblay's niece, — "never was union more blessed and felicitous; though after the first eight years of unmingled happiness, it was assailed by many calamities, chiefly of separation or illness, yet still mentally unbroken." Pending the arrival of funds for building the cottage in Norbury Park, they went into temporary lodgings in Phenice or Phœnix Farm, and subsequently migrated to what she calls — "a very small house in the suburbs of a very small village called Bookham" — about two miles from Mickleham. Very early in his wedded life M. D'Arblay announced his intention of taking part in the Toulon Expedition; but fortunately for his wife, his services, for reasons which do not appear, were not accepted by the Government. Upon this he settled down quietly to domesticity and gardening — in which he was apparently more energetic than expert. "Abdolonime,"[1] writes Mme. D'Arblay to her father after his first visit to the Bookham hermitage, — "'Abdolonime' [who figures her husband] has no regret but that his garden was not in better order; he was a little *piqué*, he confesses, that you said it was not *very neat* — and, *to be shor!* — but his passion is to do great works: he undertakes with pleasure, pursues with energy, and finishes with spirit, but, then, all is over! He thinks the business once done always done; and to repair, and amend, and weed, and cleanse, — O, these are drudgeries insupportable to him!" However, he seems to have succeeded in "*plantant des choux*," as it is admitted that the Bookham cabbages were remarkable for fresh-

[1] *Abdolonime* is a gardener of Sidon in a five act comedy by M. de Fontenelle.

ness and flavour; and when La Fayette's ex-adjutant mowed down the hedge with his sabre, his wife was "the most *contente personne* in the world" to see that warlike weapon so peaceably employed. Madame herself, after composing a not very persuasive Address to the Ladies of England on behalf of the Emigrant French clergy, was plying her pen upon a new novel and a tragedy. Then, at the close of 1794, — a year which has not been "blemished with one regretful moment," her activities were interrupted by the birth (Dec. 18) of a son, who was christened Alexandre Charles Louis Piochard, his *prénoms* being derived from his father, and his godfathers, Dr. Burney junior, and the Count de Narbonne.

The tragedy was the earlier of Mme. D'Arblay's new works to see the light. She had begun it, she says, at Kew, and she finished it at Windsor (August, 1790), without any specific intention either of production or publication. Having been read by some of her family and friends, it was shown by her brother Charles to John Kemble, who pronounced for its acceptance. A few days before the birth of her son it was suddenly required for Sheridan's inspection, with the result that, according to the author's account, it was brought out at Drury Lane without the full revision she intended, and as she subsequently had a seven weeks' illness, was never in a position, to give it. On the 21st March, 1795, it was played. But not even the Kembles and Mrs. Siddons, aided as they were by Bensley and Palmer, could secure a success for *Edwy and Elgiva*, nor could the fact that there were no fewer than three Bishops among the *dramatis personæ*, save it from being withdrawn, nominally "for

alterations," after one solitary performance. Mme.
D'Arblay quite reasonably attributes some of its ill-
fortune to her inability to correct it and superintend
the rehearsals ; and, in a later letter, which gives an
account of its fate, she lays stress upon the very
unsatisfactory acting of some of the subordinate
performers. But though *Edwy and Elgiva* was
never printed, the MS., which still exists, has been
carefully examined by a capable critic, whose report
leaves little room for doubt as to the real cause of its
faint reception.[1] Though at some points there is a
certain stir and action, the plot generally lacks incident
and movement. But what is said to be fatal is the
"incurable poverty of its stilted language, its common-
place sentiments, and its incorrect and inharmonious
versification." The specimens given of the blank verse
are certainly of the most unhappy kind. From the
fact that the MS. is carefully pencilled with amend-
ments in French and English, it is probable that, just
as "Daddy "Crisp had, to the last, believed in *Virginia*,
the author must have continued to believe in *Edwy and
Elgiva*. But though Cumberland — always forgiving
to a failure — professed that the players had lent it an
ill-name, and offered to risk his life on its success if it
were re-cast and submitted to his inspection, it is not
likely the audience were radically wrong. What is
wonderful is, that Sheridan and Kemble should have
accepted it, and that Mrs. Siddons should have consented to play the heroine.

When, a month after the production of *Edwy and
Elgiva*, Warren Hastings, to Mme. D'Arblay's great

[1] Mr. E. S. Shuckburgh, in *Macmillan's Magazine* for February, 1890, pp. 291-98.

delight, was finally acquitted, she was apparently hard at work upon her new novel, with which she makes as rapid progress as is consistent with the absorbing care of the little personage whom she styles the "Bambino," and to whom she hopes "it may be a little portion." In June she tells a friend that it has been a long time in hand, and will be published in about a year. But, owing to the expenses of the press, she has now — money being a very definite object — decided to act upon the advice, formerly given to her by Burke, and to print by subscription. "This is in many — many ways," she writes, "unpleasant and unpalatable to us both; but the chance of real use and benefit to our little darling overcomes all scruples, and, therefore, to work we go." The Honble. Mrs. Boscawen, Mrs. Crewe and Mrs. Locke consented to keep the subscription books. The result of this contrivance, which Dr. Burney (who was generally unfortunate as an adviser) did not at first approve, was a complete pecuniary success. *Camilla; or, a Picture of Youth*, was issued in the middle of 1796, in five volumes, 8vo., with a list of subscribers rivalling that of Prior to the poems of 1718. It occupies thirty-eight pages; and the whole is headed by the Duchess of York, and the Duke of Gloucester. The volumes are dedicated, from Bookham, to the Queen, who, when they were presented to her at Windsor by Mme. D'Arblay and her husband in person, repaid the compliment by a purse of one hundred guineas from herself and the King. Many persons took more than one copy. Warren Hastings interested himself specially for his staunch adherent, and engaged to attack the East Indies on her behalf. Burke, a sad and mourning man, who had lost both son and brother, subscribed nevertheless for them, as well as for his wife, sending £20 for a single copy; three of the Miss Thrales took ten copies, Mrs. Piozzi two, and so forth. It would be idle to select further names; but two are of special interest. One is that of "Miss J. Austen, Steventon"; the other that of the sworn adversary of "what you call stuff," Mrs. Schwellenberg, who with Miss Planta and Miss Goldsworthy, rallied round an old colleague. The names of Colonel Digby and his wife are significantly absent.[1] The result of all this effort was encouraging. About a month after publication Dr. Burney told Horace Walpole that his daughter had made £2000; and three months after publication only five hundred copies remained out of four thousand. The selling price was one guinea, so that Macaulay's estimate that the author "cleared more than three thousand guineas" is, — allowing for fancy payments and the Queen's *douceur*, and deducting for the cost of publication, — probably below the mark upon this occasion.

Camilla, however, could not be called a literary success, even by its contemporaries, and certainly was not an advance upon the writer's previous works. Horace Walpole, who had regretted the live-burial of the author's talents in the Windsor antechambers, was too frank to disguise his disappointment. He had not cared for *Cecilia* as much as *Evelina:* he thought the

---

[1] Mrs. Ellis thought she detected in *Camilla* a shaft aimed at the philandering Colonel. "They [men] are not like us, Lavinia. They think themselves free, if they have made no verbal profession ; though they may have pledged themselves by looks, by actions, by attentions, and by manners, a thousand, and a thousand times" (*Camilla*, 1796, iv. 42-3).

"deplorable *Camilla*" infinitely worse than *Cecilia*.
"Madame D'Arblay," — he wrote to Hannah More in
August, 1796, — had "reversed experience." She had
known the world and penetrated character before she
had stepped over the threshold, "and, now she had
seen so much of it, she had little or no insight at all."
This, of course, did not prevent the *Monthly Review*
from politely comparing her to Homer, — both for
occasionally nodding and for the peculiar distinctness
and propriety of her delineations of character. But
though Mme. D'Arblay still deserves the praise which
Burke had formerly given to her, and which the *Monthly
Review* repeats, of assigning " to each person a language
of his own, and preserving it uniformly through the
work," the maze of misapprehensions which encompass
the loves of Camilla Tyrold and Edgar Mandlebert grows
sadly tedious, and the book, it must be confessed, is
difficult reading. Whether, if it had been written in
the style of *Evelina*, it would have been more attractive, is impossible to say: the style in which it is in
great part written, by reason of its absurd roundabout
pomposity, is simply unendurable. " Where opinion
may humour systematic prepossession, who shall build
upon his virtue or wisdom to guard the transparency
of his impartiality " — is one of the sentences which
even Mr. Griffiths' review is forced to characterise
as "singularly obscure." Obscure it certainly is; but
it is not by any means single, for there are other
passages to pattern. For this extraordinary degradation of manner various reasons have been assigned.
It has been ascribed to recollections of Johnson, — to
imitation of Dr. Burney, — to the influence of a French
husband, — to the inflation superinduced upon a court

appointment.   There is another cause that has not
been mentioned, which we suspect had more to do with
the matter than any of the things suggested.   This
is, that Mme. D'Arblay had recently been engaged in
the composing of much indifferent blank verse ; and
like other distinguished authors, she fell insensibly
into this laboured style whenever she had anything
to say in her own person which she regarded as
unusually fine.   And it is curious that the manner
must have been adopted *de parti pris*, for, as the
" Abdolonime " quotation on an earlier page almost
suffices to show, she was, at this very time, writing
easy and graphic letters to her friends.   But apart
from the style, and the fact that the personages re-
produce, in many instances, the earlier types, there
is still humour and careful character-drawing in the
Orkbornes and Dubsters and Clarendels of *Camilla*.
And even the impatient modern may care to remember
that in Chapter V. of *Northanger Abbey* Jane Austen
does not scruple to couple it with *Cecilia* and Miss
Edgeworth's *Belinda* in terms of enthusiastic praise ;
and that Charles Lamb himself in a sonnet to Fanny's
novelist step-sister Sarah Harriet, referring to her
elder as —

> " renowned for many a tale
> Of faithful love perplexed " —

goes on to commend specially the character of Sir
Hugh Tyrold —

> " that good
> Old man, who, as CAMILLA's guardian, stood
> In obstinate virtue clad like coat of mail." [1]

---

[1] Lamb's sonnet was first published in the *Morning Chronicle*,
13th July, 1820, upon the appearance of Sarah Burney's tale of

At the close of 1796 Mme. D'Arblay lost her step-mother. By this time she was apparently engaged in converting the gains from *Camilla* into bricks and mortar. Upon a piece of land in a field at West Humble, leased to her husband by Mr. Locke of Norbury,[1] they built a cottage, to which, at Dr. Burney's suggestion, they gave the name of the novel;[2] and the letters at this date are full of the activities of M. D'Arblay, who was his own sole architect and surveyor, in planning his new garden, digging a well, and constructing a sunk fence to prevent the inroads of the domestic (and prospective) cow. As may be anticipated, the cost of building largely exceeded the estimate. "Our new habitation" — she writes in August, 1797 — "will very considerably indeed exceed our first intentions and expectations"; and not much remained when the bills for Camilla Cottage were discharged. The expenses of living in war time, too, were exceptionally heavy, and various expedients were

Country Neighbours. The author is indebted for knowledge of this poem to the courtesy of Mr. E. V. Lucas, at pp. 82–3, vol. v., of whose very valuable edition of Lamb's works it is printed. Lamb also addressed a sonnet to Martin Charles Burney, Admiral Burney's son. It is prefixed to vol. ii. of his *Works*, 1818. Martin Burney, a barrister, and a dear friend of Lamb, is also mentioned in Elia's "Detached Thoughts on Books and Reading." His mother is thought to have been "Mrs. Battle."

[1] For reasons connected with the future tenancy of the house, Mr. Locke's offer of a site in Norbury Park itself had finally been declined.

[2] The house, Camilla Lacey, still exists ; but altered and en-larged. When Thorne wrote his *Environs of London* in 1876, it belonged to Mr. J. L. Wylie, and contained many interesting Burney relics. It is now in possession of Mr. Wylie's nephew, Mr. F. Leverton Harris, M.P. for Tynemouth.

suggested to replenish the *pot-au-feu*, including the liberal planting of potatoes in every corner of the little property. It was perhaps wise that under this pressure Mme. D'Arblay did not fall in with Mrs. Crewe's proposal that she should edit an Anti-Jacobin journal to be styled *The Breakfast Table.* But she again attempted the stage with a comedy called *Love and Fashion*, which, in 1799, was actually accepted and put into rehearsal by Harris of Covent Garden. Dr. Burney, however, had set his heart upon fiction. It was in vain that his daughter protested that all her life she had been urged to write a comedy, and that to write a comedy was her ambition. Moreover, that the incidents and effects for a drama occurred to her, and the combinations for a long work did not. Her father was seized with a panic of failure, and early in 1800 *Love and Fashion* was hastily withdrawn. Before this took place, Mme. D'Arblay had the misfortune to lose her sister, Mrs. Phillips, who since 1796 had been resident in Ireland. She died on the 6th January, when on her way to visit her relations. In 1801, the preliminaries for the short-lived Peace of Amiens having been signed, and the difficulties of the domestic situation being urgent, M. D'Arblay decided to return to France, hoping vaguely, first, to recover his lost property, and, secondly, to obtain from Napoleon something in the nature of a recognition of his past military services. Ultimately, having stipulated that he should not be called upon to serve against his wife's country, and having besides pledged himself to the Alien office, when obtaining his passport, not to return to that country for a year, he found himself in the double predicament of getting nothing, and being obliged to remain in France, whither he accordingly summoned his *bonne amie* and his son.

Mme. D'Arblay expected to have been able to come back to her father in eighteen months : she stayed in France ten years. During this period she resided with her husband at Passy. Their means, in the absence of remittances from England, which had practically ceased with the renewal of the war, consisted, primarily, of a small military *retraite*, or retiring allowance, of 1500 francs per annum (£62, 10s.), and later of a modest income earned by M. D'Arblay as a *rédacteur* and afterwards *sous-chef* in the Civil Department of *les Bâtiments* (*Ministère de l'Intérieur*). The post was no sinecure, and carried him to Paris daily from about half-past eight to half-past five. But he was treated by his chiefs with exemplary good feeling and consideration ; and although, for lack of funds, only three rooms of the little home in the Rue Basse were finished and furnished, the husband and wife were perfectly happy. " Our view is extremely pretty from it [Paris on one side; the country on the other], and always cheerful; we rarely go out, yet always are pleased to return. We have our books, our prate, and our boy — how, with all this, can we, or ought we, to suffer ourselves to complain of our narrowed and narrowing income ? " This was written in April, 1804. In 1810, they have apparently moved to Paris, for she dates from the Rue D'Anjou ; and is rejoicing over the adopted friends she has found in her adopted country. " The society in which I mix, when I can prevail with myself to quit my yet dearer fireside, is all that can be wished, whether for wit, wisdom, intelligence, gaiety or politeness. M. D'Arblay, says the same letter, is

well, and at his office, where he is sadly overworked;
and their son, now a youth of fifteen, with mathematical
gifts, is preparing, at the same table, an exercise for
his master. He is thin, pale and strong — we are
told elsewhere; — but terribly *sauvage*, and singularly
"averse to all the forms of society. Where he can
have got such a rebel humour we conceive not; but
it costs him more to make a bow than to resolve six
difficult problems of algebra, or to repeat twelve pages
from Euripides; and as to making a civil speech, he
would sooner renounce the world." [1]

In 1810 M. D'Arblay yielded to his wife's desire to
visit her friends in England. Everything had been
done, and M. de Narbonne had procured her passport
from the terrible Fouché, when a sudden embargo
blocked all departures from the coast, and she was
unable to start. In the following year she was
operated upon for "a menace of cancer" by Napoleon's
famous surgeon, Baron de Larrey, a trial which, according to her niece, she bore with such fortitude as
to earn, in her French circle, the name of *L'Ange*. In
1812 she made another, and a more successful, attempt
to reach England. The necessity was then growing
urgent, as her son was seventeen, and liable soon to
a conscription which would have forced him to do
the very thing his father had endeavoured to avoid,
— namely, to fight the English. Mme. D'Arblay and
young Alexandre, after waiting six weeks vainly at

[1] In "A Burney Friendship" (*Side-Lights on the Georgian
Period*, by George Paston, 1902, pp. 31-32), there is an interesting extract from one of Mme. D'Arblay's letters describing
the young Alexandre's triumphs at "the principal *école* of
Passy."

Dunkirk, at last landed at Deal in August. Many things had happened in her ten years' absence. The King was now hopelessly mad; the Princess Amelia was dead; Mr. Twining was dead, as was also Mr. Locke of Norbury. She found her father sadly aged and broken, and indeed almost entirely confined to his bedroom. But she had plenty to occupy her during her stay. First, there was the settling of her son at Cambridge, where, having gained the Tancred scholarship, he began residence at Christ's College in October 1813. Then there was the completion and publication of a new book, of which nearly three volumes out of five had been finished before she quitted France. Already, from Paris, she had been attempting some informal negotiations as to this, for Byron had heard of its existence. " My bookseller, Cawthorne," — he wrote to Harness in Dec. 1811, — "has just left me, and tells me, with a most important face, that he is in treaty for a novel of Madame D'Arblay's, for which 1000 guineas are asked! He wants me to read the MS. (if he obtains it), which I shall do with pleasure; but I should be very cautious in venturing an opinion on her whose *Cecilia* Dr. Johnson superintended.[1] If he lends it to me, I shall put it into the hands of Rogers and M[oor]e, who are truly men of taste." Three days later, he repeats the story to Hodgson; but the amount has grown to 1500 guineas.

The best one can say about *The Wanderer; or,*

---

[1] Moore's *Life of Lord Byron*, 1844, 147. Moore corrects this in a note. But it shows that Johnson's alleged revision of *Cecilia* must have been current as a rumour long before Macaulay asserted it upon internal evidence in 1843.

Female Difficulties, issued in March 1814, is, that it
brought grist to the mill. It was not published by
subscription like *Camilla;* [1] but Mme. D'Arblay herself
tells us that 3600 copies were "positively sold and
paid for" at the "rapacious price" of two guineas each
in six months. From a literary point of view the
book was an utter failure. It "was apparently never
read by anybody," observes Sir Leslie Stephen; and
Macaulay says that "no judicious friend to the author's
memory will attempt to draw it from the oblivion into
which it has justly fallen." Even Mme. D'Arblay's
most faithful editor and admirer, Mrs. Ellis, makes
open and heartfelt thanksgiving that it is not her
duty to read it again. After these discouraging
opinions from critics not unfriendly, it is scarcely sur-
prising to learn that *The Wanderer* was attacked with
unusual severity in the *Quarterly* for April, 1814; or
that Hazlitt should, in the *Edinburgh* for February,
1815, make it the sorry pretext for that admirable
survey of the national fiction which he afterwards
converted into No. VI. of his *Lectures on the English
Comic Writers.* Hazlitt earned, as has already been told
in chapter i., the disapprobation of honest James Burney for his treatment of Mme. D'Arblay's final effort.
Yet it is notable that the critic blames *The Wanderer,*
not for "decay of talent, but a perversion of it." It
is impossible to say as much now. The book, in truth,
is wearisome, and its "difficulties" are unreal. The
reason for its first success is, we suspect, to be traced to
the cause suggested by Mme. D'Arblay herself, namely,

[1] The arrangement was, that she was to receive £1500 in three
payments, spread over a year and a half. If 8000 copies were sold
she was to have £3000.

the prevailing expectation that its pages would present a picture of contemporary and revolutionary France, where, it was known, the writer had been residing; and that this led to copies being freely bespoken beforehand. When the real nature of its theme — the trivial and improbable adventures, in England, of a female refugee during the reign of Robespierre — was fully appreciated, the sale immediately fell off. Were it not futile, it would be interesting to speculate whether, had *The Wanderer* taken the place of *Evelina* in the order of Mme. D'Arblay's productions, it would have succeeded at all, even in the absence of rivals. But it is a curious instance of the irony of circumstance that a book which nobody could read should have brought more than £7000 to somebody in the year in which Miss Edgeworth published *Patronage*, and Miss Austen, *Mansfield Park*. It is also more curious still, that in this very year Constable could not see his way to risk more than £700 on the copyright of an anonymous novel entitled *Waverley ; or, 'tis Sixty Years Since.*

The Preface or Dedication to *The Wanderer*, from which some quotations have already been made during the progress of this volume, is dated 14 March, 1814. On the 12 April following, Dr. Burney died, being nursed tenderly by his daughter Fanny during his last illness. He had attained his eighty-eighth year, and since 1806 had enjoyed a pension of £300 per annum. One of the last distinctions of his busy career, which he had latterly occupied with a *Life of Metastasio* and contributions to Rees' *Cyclopædia*, was that of Correspondent to the Institute of France, the diploma for which Mme. D'Arblay brought with her from

Paris. A tablet was erected to his memory in Westminster Abbey. Not long after his death, his daughter had the honour of being presented, in England, to Louis XVIII., who received her effusively, complimenting her, "in very pretty English," upon her writings, and bidding her farewell at last under the style of "Madame la Comtesse."[1] This was in April, 1814, after the taking of Paris, and the abdication of Buonaparte. A short time subsequently M. D'Arblay arrived from the French capital. He received a commission from the Duc de Luxembourg as Sous-Lieutenant in the Corps de Garde, and was restored to his old rank as Maréchal de Camp. He came to England on leave later in the same year, and took his wife back with him to France. Then followed the return of Buonaparte from Elba; and in March, 1815, Mme. D'Arblay took flight for Brussels. Some time afterwards she wrote from memory a narrative of the Hundred Days (March 20 to June 28), which has interest, but not the interest of a journal, although it is supposed to have supplied Thackeray with hints for the Brussels chapters of *Vanity Fair*. In July of the same year, General D'Arblay, while attempting, at Trèves, to raise a troop of refugees, received a kick

---

[1] She never used this title — as she says in an unpublished letter, dated 26 June, 1827, to her nephew, Dr. C. P. Burney, where she adds to her signature, "otherwise La Comtesse Veuve Piochard D'Arblay" — "because I have had no Fortune to meet it, and because my Son relinquished his hereditary claims of succession — though he might, upon certain conditions, resume them — on becoming a Clergyman of the Church of England. But I have never *dis*claimed *my* Rights, as I owe them to no Honours of my own, but to a Partnership in those which belonged to the revered Husband who, for twenty-four years, made the grateful Happiness of my Life."

from an unbroken horse. The accident was made
worse by unskilled surgery; and having now, like his
wife, passed his sixtieth year, he was placed on the
retired list, with the title of Lieutenant-General, and
received permission to settle in England. Three years
later (3 May, 1818), he died at Bath, being buried in
Walcot churchyard.[1] General D'Arblay is one of the
most delightful figures in his wife's *Diary*. A true
militaire — as Susan Burney called him — he is also a
typical specimen of the old pre-revolutionary *régime*,
courteous, cheerful, amiable, and as dignified in ill-
fortune as he is patient under poverty.

The remaining occurrences of Mme. D'Arblay's life
may be rapidly related. At Bath, in 1817, she had
renewed her acquaintance with Mrs. Piozzi. At Ilfra-
combe, in the same year, she had a narrow escape from
drowning, being surprised by the rising of the tide
when she was searching for curiosities. After M.
D'Arblay's death she moved to 11, Bolton Street,
Piccadilly, which bears a Society of Arts tablet in
testimony of her residence there. It was at Bolton
Street that she was visited by Sir Walter Scott, who
describes her in his *Journal* for Nov. 18, 1826.
Rogers took him. He found her an elderly lady (she
was then seventy-four), " with no remains of personal
beauty, but with a gentle manner and a pleasing
expression of countenance." " She told me she had
wished to see two persons — myself, of course, being
one; the other, George Canning. This was really a
compliment to be pleased with — a nice little handsome
pat of butter made up by a neat-handed Phillis of a

---

[1] In the previous year Mme. D'Arblay had lost her brother
Charles. James, the Admiral, survived to 1821.

dairymaid, instead of the grease, fit only for cart-wheels, which one is dosed with by the pound." She told him the story of *Evelina*, and the mulberry tree episode.[1] "I trust I shall see this lady again," writes Scott; "she has simple and apparently amiable manners, with quick feelings."[2] He did see her again, two years later, and again with Rogers, when she showed him some notes which she induced him to believe had been recollected and jotted down in compliance with his suggestion on the former occasion. This was in May 1828.[3]

From 1828 to 1832 she busied herself in putting together the *Memoirs of Dr. Burney*, which appeared in the latter year. They are based, with slight exceptions, on her father's own MSS., drawn up in 1807 and afterwards, and on her own unprinted diaries and personal recollections. She herself was eighty when they were published, and her style had not improved with age. For the present generation, these records have been superseded by the publication of the original diaries and letters upon which in part they were based; but when they were issued in 1832, their memories and anecdotes were new to the public, who were not so impatient of their other defects as are later readers. Southey, indeed, to whom the volumes were sent by the author's son, was unreserved in his praise. He wrote from Keswick that *Evelina* had not

---

[1] See *ante*, p. 87.

[2] *Journal of Sir Walter Scott*, 1891, i. 308–9. Rogers' *Table Talk*, 1856, p. 192, adds a detail of the first visit. Mme. D'Arblay had not heard that Scott was lame; and, seeing him limp, hoped he had not met with an accident. He answered, "An accident, Madam, nearly as old as my birth."

[3] *Ibid.* ii. 190.

given him more pleasure when he was a schoolboy than these memoirs had given him now, and that was saying a good deal. "Except Boswell's" — he went on — "there is no other work in our language which carries us into such society, and makes us fancy that we are acquainted with the people to whom we are there introduced." But Croker, whom she had declined to assist with material for his edition of Boswell, made the *Memoirs* the subject of malignant attack in the *Quarterly* for April, 1833. Mme. D'Arblay — we are given to understand — was seriously pained by the imputation of unveracity contained in this article; and she might well be hurt on other grounds. The duties of reviewers are not always pleasant to perform; and Croker might plead, in defence of his ungallant inquisition into the author's age, that, like Rousseau, he was simply actuated by the love of truth; but to say of a blameless and inoffensive old lady of eighty, who might certainly claim indulgence for imperfect recollection, that her style could not have been "more feeble, anile, incoherent, or *'sentant plus l'apoplexie,'*" is surely to write oneself down both cruel and contemptible.

One of the rare references to Mme. D'Arblay at this date is contained in Disraeli's letters to his sister. "*Contarini*," he writes, "seems universally liked, but moves slowly. The staunchest admirer I have in London, and the most discerning appreciator of *Contarini*, is old Madame D'Arblay. I have a long letter, which I will show you, — capital!" This was written in July, 1832. In 1837 Mme. D'Arblay had the misfortune to lose her son. Since she had placed him at Cambridge in 1813, he had done well. He had graduated in 1818 as tenth Wrangler; and though handicapped by a French education, became a Fellow of his College (Christ's). Having taken orders in 1819, he was made, in 1836, minister of Ely Chapel, Holborn. He was preparing to marry, when he succumbed suddenly to influenza in January, 1837. His mother did not long survive him. Two years later, she was attacked by an illness, which was accompanied by spectral illusions; and, on January 6, 1840, being then in her eighty-eighth year, she died, at Lower Grosvenor Street, New Bond Street, and was buried by the side of her husband and son at Walcot. The prettiest story of her last days is told by Rogers. It is *à propos* of the well-known lines which begin —

"Life! we 've been long together";

and end —

"Say not Good Night, but in some brighter clime
Bid me Good Morning."

"Sitting with Madame D'Arblay some time before she died, I [Rogers] said to her, 'Do you remember those lines of Mrs. Barbauld's *Life*, which I once repeated to you?' 'Remember them,' she replied; 'I repeat them to myself every night before I go to sleep.'"[1]

In 1842, two years after Mme. D'Arblay's death, the first five volumes of her *Diary and Letters* were issued. These, like the *Memoirs of Dr. Burney*, were savagely assailed by Croker in the *Quarterly* in an article which had the good fortune to provoke a masterly retort in the *Edinburgh* from Lord Macaulay. Modern research has rectified some of the minor de-

[1] *Table Talk of Samuel Rogers*, 1856, 179–80.

tails, and modern criticism may dissent from some of the deductions, in this famous counterblast. But though no doubt prompted by antagonism to Mme. D'Arblay's assailant in the rival review, and though strongly coloured by the writer's political opinions, it remains, and must remain, a memorable tribute to the author of *Evelina* and *Cecilia*.

To Lord Macaulay's essay, indeed, and to its periodical reproduction in fresh editions of his works, is probably due most of Mme. D'Arblay's existing reputation as a novelist. And that reputation rests almost exclusively upon her first two productions, *Evelina* and *Cecilia*. We doubt if the piety of the enthusiast could ever revive — or rather create — the slightest interest in *The Wanderer ;* or that any but the fanatics of the out-of-date, or the student of manners, could conscientiously struggle through *Camilla*. Works of genius, it is true, are occasionally born out of due time, and consequently fail of the recognition they deserve from their contemporaries, only to attain it eventually either through the insight of the independent critic, or the better knowledge of after ages. But these were not the circumstances of *Camilla* and *The Wanderer*. Both books were circulated freely among an audience not only specially qualified to judge, but also specially well-disposed; and if, with these advantages, they could not succeed in obtaining approbation, it is idle to attempt to revive them now. With *Cecilia* and *Evelina*, the case is different. They stand on their merits. And their merits are undeniable. It is true that — as Walpole said — *Cecilia* is too long ; but its crowd of characters is very skilfully varied, and many of them, as Briggs, Albany, Mr.

Delville, Mrs. Harrel, Mr. Monckton, are drawn with marked ability. And though the book has less freshness than its predecessor, it has more constructive power and greater certainty of hand. Mme. D'Arblay's masterpiece, however, is *Evelina*. This she wrote because she must, — neither preoccupied with her public nor her past;[1] — and throughout this book penned for amusement in Newton's old observatory, one never catches, as in *Cecilia*, the creak of the machinery, or fancies, in the background, the paternal voice pressing for prompt publication. It is perhaps difficult for a modern reader to be impressed by the sentiments of the excellent Mr. Villars, still less to "blubber," like Dr. Burney, over Sir John Belmont's heroics; but, in spite of youthful exaggerations and faults of taste, it is still possible to admire the vivacity with which Miss Anville narrates her experiences, embarrassments, and social trepidations. It is also possible to comprehend something of the unparalleled enthusiasm produced by the opportune appearance of Evelina's history in a dead season of letters — by its freedom from taint of immorality, its unfeigned fun and humour, and its unhackneyed descriptions of humanity. One can easily conceive how welcome these latter characteristics must have been to a public sickened and depressed by the "inflammatory tales" and "sentimental frippery"[2] of the circulating libraries. *Evelina*, moreover, marks

---

[1] "It was not hard fagging that produced such a work as *Evelina*" — wrote "Daddy" Crisp in 1779 — "it was the ebullition of true sterling genius — you wrote it because you could not help it — it came, and so you put it down on paper." (*Diary and Letters*, 1892, i. 178.)

[2] These expressions are from Cowper's *Progress of Error*, written in 1780–1.

a definite deviation in the progress of the national fiction. Leaving Fielding's breezy and bustling highway, leaving the analytic hothouse of Richardson, it carries the novel of manners into domestic life, and prepares the way for Miss Edgeworth and the exquisite parlour-pieces of Miss Austen.

Of the *Memoirs of Dr. Burney*, it is not necessary to say much more than has already been said. Although, as we have seen, Southey could praise them warmly, — to be sure, he was acknowledging a complimentary copy, — Macaulay declares that they were received with "a cry of disgust," which a later writer converts into "a scream of derision." Yet it must nevertheless be admitted that they contain much in the way of letters, documents, and anecdote which the student cannot well neglect; and it should be observed that it is in the connecting passages that the writer's "peculiar rhetoric" is most manifest. The curious expedients she adopts to avoid using the personal pronoun; and the catenated phrases to which Croker objected, and which he unkindly emphasised by hyphens (*e.g.* "the yet very handsome though no longer in her bloom, Mrs. Stephen Allen," "the sudden, at the moment, though from lingering illnesses often previously expected death, of Mrs. Burney "), — are certainly amusing; as is also the nebulous magniloquence of passages like the following, not, it may be added, an exceptional specimen : — "This sharp infliction, however, though it ill recompensed his ethereal flight, by no means checked his literary ambition; and the ardour which was cooled for gazing at the stars, soon seemed doubly re-animated for the music of the spheres." But what is more extraordinary than these utterances is, that

Mme. D'Arblay seems herself to have had no suspicion of their extravagance, since we find her, even
after the publication of *The Wanderer*, gravely enjoining her son to avoid overstrained expression, not to
labour to embellish his thoughts, and above all, to "be
natural." [1]

Happily for her readers, the *Diary* — to which we
now come — is not written in the pernicious style of the
Memoirs of Dr. Burney. Even in those parts of it which
were composed after *Cecilia* and *Camilla*, it is still clear,
fluent, and unaffected. Now and then, perhaps, — as
in the quotation on Burke's oratory at p. 160, — there is
a sense of effort; but in general, the manner is delightful. Why Macaulay, who praised the *Diary* so much,
did not praise it more, — did not, in fact, place it high
above Mme. D'Arblay's efforts as a novelist, — is hard
to comprehend. It has all the graphic picturesqueness,
all the dramatic interest, all the objective characteri-
sation, all the happy faculty of "making her descriptions alive" (as "Daddy" Crisp had said), — which
constitute the charm of the best passages in *Evelina*.
But it has the further advantage that it is true;
and that it deals with real people. King George
and Queen Charlotte, Mrs. Schwellenberg and M.
de Guiffardière, Johnson and Reynolds, Burke and
Garrick, Sheridan, Cumberland, Mrs. Thrale, Mrs.
Delany, Omai and Count Orloff — stand before us in
their habits as they lived, and we know them more
intimately than Mr. Briggs, believe in them more
implicitly than in Captain Mirvan, and laugh at them
more honestly than at "Madam French." The *Diary* of
Mme. D'Arblay deserves to rank with the great diaries

[1] *Diary and Letters*, 1892, iv. 339.

of literature. It is nothing that it is egotistical, for egotism is of its essence ; it is nothing that it is minute, its minuteness enforces the impression. It gives us a gallery of portraits which speak and move ; and a picture of society which we recognise as substantially true to life.

INDEX

ENGLISH MEN OF LETTERS

EDITED BY

JOHN MORLEY

Cloth. 12mo. Price, 40 cents, each

ADDISON. By W. J. Courthope.

BACON. By R. W. Church.

BENTLEY. By Prof. Jebb.

BUNYAN. By J. A. Froude.

BURKE. By John Morley.

BURNS. By Principal Shairp.

BYRON. By Prof. Nichol.

CARLYLE. By Prof. Nichol.

CHAUCER. By Prof. A. W. Ward.

COLERIDGE. By H. D. Traill.

COWPER. By Goldwin Smith.

DEFOE. By W. Minto.

DE QUINCEY. By Prof. Masson.

DICKENS. By A. W. Ward.

DRYDEN. By G. Saintsbury.

FIELDING. By Austin Dobson.

GIBBON. By J. Cotter Morison.

GOLDSMITH. By William Black.

GRAY. By Edmund Gosse.

HUME. By T. H. Huxley.

JOHNSON. By Leslie Stephen.

KEATS. By Sidney Colvin.

LAMB. By Alfred Ainger.

LANDOR. By Sidney Colvin.

LOCKE. By Prof. Fowler.

MACAULAY.
By J. Cotter Morison.

MILTON. By Mark Pattison.

POPE. By Leslie Stephen.

SCOTT. By R. H. Hutton.

SHELLEY. By J. A. Symonds.

SHERIDAN. By Mrs. Oliphant.

SIR PHILIP SIDNEY.
By J. A. Symonds.

SOUTHEY. By Prof. Dowden.

SPENSER. By R. W. Church.

STERNE. By H. D. Traill.

SWIFT. By Leslie Stephen.

THACKERAY. By A. Trollope.

WORDSWORTH.
By F. W. H. Myers.

NEW VOLUMES

Cloth. 12mo. Price, 75 cents net

GEORGE ELIOT. By Leslie Stephen.

WILLIAM HAZLITT. By Augustine Birrell.

MATTHEW ARNOLD. By Herbert W. Paul.

JOHN RUSKIN. By Frederic Harrison.

JOHN GREENLEAF WHITTIER. By Thomas W. Higginson.

ALFRED TENNYSON. By Alfred Lyall.

SAMUEL RICHARDSON. By Austin Dobson.

ROBERT BROWNING. By G. K. Chesterton.

CRABBE. By Alfred Ainger.

ENGLISH MEN OF LETTERS

EDITED BY

JOHN MORLEY

THREE BIOGRAPHIES IN EACH VOLUME

Cloth. 12mo. Price, $1.00, each

CHAUCER. By Adolphus William Ward. **SPENSER.** By R. W. Church. **DRYDEN.** By George Saintsbury.

MILTON. By Mark Pattison, B.D. **GOLDSMITH.** By William Black. **COWPER.** By Goldwin Smith.

BYRON. By John Nichol. **SHELLEY.** By John Addington Symonds. **KEATS.** By Sidney Colvin, M.A.

WORDSWORTH. By F. W. H. Myers. **SOUTHEY.** By Edward Dowden. **LANDOR.** By Sidney Colvin, M.A.

LAMB. By Alfred Ainger. **ADDISON.** By W. J. Courthope. **SWIFT.** By Leslie Stephen.

SCOTT. By Richard H. Hutton. **BURNS.** By Principal Shairp. **COLERIDGE.** By H. D. Traill.

HUME. By T. H. Huxley, F.R.S. **LOCKE.** By Thomas Fowler. **BURKE.** By John Morley.

FIELDING. By Austin Dobson. **THACKERAY.** By Anthony Trollope. **DICKENS.** By Adolphus William Ward.

GIBBON. By J. Cotter Morison. **CARLYLE.** By John Nichol. **MACAULAY.** By J. Cotter Morison.

SIDNEY. By J. A. Symonds. **DE QUINCEY.** By David Masson. **SHERIDAN.** By Mrs. Oliphant.

POPE. By Leslie Stephen. **JOHNSON.** By Leslie Stephen. **GRAY.** By Edmund Gosse.

BACON. By R. W. Church. **BUNYAN.** By J. A. Froude. **BENTLEY.** By R. C. Jebb.

PUBLISHED BY

THE MACMILLAN COMPANY

66 FIFTH AVENUE, NEW YORK